# nerife

**La Orotava.** La Orotava's Casa de los Balcones is the best example of a traditional town mansion. See page 47.

**Masca.** A dramatically-located village with a challenging hike down to the sea. See page 67.

**El Teide.** This dramatic, snowcapped volcano is Spain's highest mountain. See page 54.

**Castillo de San Miguel.** The castle in Garachico has great views out to sea. See page 64.

**San Cristóbal de la Laguna.** With many lovely old buildings, the former capital is a Unesco World Heritage Site. See page 36.

**Siam Park.** The Thai-themed water kingdom is one of the most spectacular aquatic parks in Europe. See page 73.

**Museo de la Naturaleza y el Hombre.** Located in Santa Cruz, this is Tenerife's largest museum. See page 31.

**Los Gigantes.** Beneath sheer cliffs that give it its name, the resort is a major centre for diving and boat trips. See page 69.

**Whale-watching.** Seeing pilot whales and bottle-nosed dolphins between Tenerife and La Gomera is an unforgettable experience. See page 88.

**Parque Etnográfico Pirámides de Güímar.** These structures are thought to be pyramids built for sun worship. See page 78.

# A PERFECT DAY

**9am** **Breakfast**

Soak up the sea views at Playa de las Vistas and breakfast at the Water Melon (Centro Comercial San Telmo) in San Telmo, Los Cristianos.

**11.30am** **Arguayo**

Rejoin the main road going north. After Chio head right via the village of Arguayo, home to the Museum of 'Cha Domitila' (tel: 922 863 465), where you can watch potters at work and purchase ceramics.

**12.30pm** **Masca**

Carry on north via Las Manchas to Santiago del Teide. From here continue to Tenerife's most picturesque village – Masca, at the head of a dramatic gorge. Enjoy the breathtaking views from one of the roadside restaurants – Chez Arlette, El Guanche (Calle El Lomito 9, tel: 922 863 027) is a good bet.

**10am** **Adeje**

Take the main TF1 road north and divert to the unspoilt hill town of Adeje, former seat of the Guanche tribe and later stronghold of the Counts of Gomera. Visit the remains of their Casa Fuerte and amble along the steep Rambla with its bars and cafés. Adeje is the entry point to the Barranca del Infierno (Hell's Gorge), a popular 4-mile (6.3km) return hike which should be saved for another day.

# IN TENERIFE

### 4pm — West Coast

Head back south on the main road, then at Tamaimo turn on to the TF454 down the valley for Los Gigantes. 'The Giants' is named after the soaring volcanic walls that drop sheer into the sea. Continue south along the coast, pausing perhaps at the fishing village-cum-beach resort of Playa de San Juan.

### 2pm — Garachico

Return to the main road and head north (TF82) for the charming coastal village of Garachico. Spend a couple of hours here, taking a dip in the lava rock pools, visiting the ex-Convent of San Francisco, admiring the views from Castillo de San Miguel or cooling off with a drink in the Plaza.

### 11pm — Nightlife

End the evening at the über-cool El Faro Chill Art (CC Torviscas Playa, tel: 922 712 842) between Puerto Colón and Fañabe Beach, watching the sun sink from the Zen terrace – before partying at the disco inside.

### 7pm — Sunset Wining and Dining

Enjoy a cocktail at La Caleta on the Costa Adeje, then tuck into superb seafood gourmet food at Restaurant 88, Masía del Mar (tel: 922 775 829; www.restaurant88tenerife.com; tel: 922 710 895) or Piscis Terraza (tel: 922 710 241), with stunning views over the Atlantic Ocean.

# CONTENTS

**Introduction** . . . . . . . . . . . . . . . . . . . . 9

**A Brief History** . . . . . . . . . . . . . . 16

**Where to Go** . . . . . . . . . . . . . . . . . 27
❶ *Numbered map references pinpoint the sights*

The Northeast . . . . . . . . . . . . . . . . . . . . . .27
*Santa Cruz de Tenerife 27, San Cristóbal La
Laguna 36, The Anaga Hills 39,*

The North Coast . . . . . . . . . . . . . . . . . . . .41
*Puerto de la Cruz 42, La Orotava 47, The wine
lands of Tacoronte 50, West of Puerto de la Cruz 52*

El Teide . . . . . . . . . . . . . . . . . . . . . . . . . .54
*Las Cañadas del Teide Crater 55, The routes into the
park 57, From the north 58, From the east 58, The
starting point 59, Cable car and Parador hotel 59,
From the southwest 61, From the west 62*

The Northwest . . . . . . . . . . . . . . . . . . . . .62
*Garachico 63, West of Garachico 66, Masca 67,
El Tanque 68, Los Gigantes to San Juan 69*

The south . . . . . . . . . . . . . . . . . . . . . . . . .70
*The big resorts 71, Los Cristianos 73, The municipal
towns 75, Along the south coast 76, Granadilla
de Abona to Güímar 77, Ancient temples 78,
Candelaria 80*

## What to Do ................... 83

Outdoor Activities ................ 83

Water Activities .................. 87

Spectator Sports................. 89

For Children .................... 90

Shopping ....................... 91

Nightlife........................ 93

Festivals........................ 95

## Eating Out ................ 98

## A–Z Travel Tips ............. 115

## Recommended Hotels...... 134

## Index ...................... 142

### Features

*Historical landmarks* ....................25

*Gentlemen at war* .......................32

*Walking in the Anaga Hills* ..............40

*The Dragon Tree* ........................52

*Climbing El Teide peak* ..................57

*Siam Park*...............................73

*La Gomera*..............................74

*Where to gamble* ........................95

*Festivals*.................................97

*Fish on the menu*........................101

# INTRODUCTION

Time signals on state radio and television in Spain give two times: one for mainland Spain and one for 'Las Canarias'. Adrift in the Atlantic Ocean more than 1,000km (620 miles) to the south of Spain, and 115km (70 miles) from the west coast of Africa, Tenerife and the 12 other islands that make up the Canary archipelago don't see the sun rise until around one hour later than their mainland compatriots.

At just over 2,000 sq km (around 800 sq miles), Tenerife is the largest of these volcanic cones that began to erupt from the depths of the Atlantic bed 20 million years ago. Six are tiny and uninhabited. Of the others, the three closest to Africa (Gran Canaria, Lanzarote and Fuerteventura) are the oldest, formed 10 million years before Tenerife. Finally, some 2 million years after that, the Canaries' other western isles of La Palma, La Gomera and El Hierro burst into life.

## Volcanic landscape

On a clear day all the islands can be seen from the top of Tenerife's Pico del Teide, which at 3,718m (12,195ft) is the highest mountain in the whole of Spain. Its peak was formed a million years ago inside the crater of a former, collapsed volcano, the Circo de Cañadas, where the landscape is burnt and hauntingly bleak. There has been no volcanic activity here for 500,000 years, though eruptions have occurred elsewhere

### Island neighbours

The nearest island to Tenerife is La Gomera 30km (18 miles) west. Gran Canaria, capital of the eastern isles, is 60km (36 miles) southeast, and the sea between them is 2,000m (6,560ft) deep.

The road to Masca winds through deep valleys

Formations at Cumbre Dorsal

on the island, the last in 1909 on Montaña Chinyero, near Santiago del Teide. Lava fields created by the volcanoes are only part of a diversity of landscapes on this island, the shape of an inverted triangle of just 2,034 sq km (785 sq miles). It includes tropical gardens, misty forests, fertile mountain slopes, tranquil villages, rocky headlands and black beaches, the most popular of which have been lined with imported Sahara sand.

## Climate

The climate on Tenerife is pleasant all year round, with little variation in the average annual temperature of around 22°C (72°F). It is this attractive climate that has made the Canaries such a popular holiday destination. The Teide massif effectively divides Tenerife into two climatic zones, north and south.

The northerly trade winds result in more cloud cover and rainfall in the north, with the coast enjoying a constant, warm, subtropical climate. Cloud conditions constantly vary, making it sometimes hard to know what to expect. Higher up, in the cloud layer between 500 and 1,200m (1,600–4,000ft), it is cooler and more humid and the sun generally shines only in the mornings. Above the cloud layer the temperatures vary greatly between day and night; in winter they drop below freezing and snow falls, creating small lakes as it melts.

The south of the island, where the popular tourist beaches have sprung up, is hot and dry, reaching almost desert conditions. Clouds are rare and there is little rainfall, but the sirocco wind from the south occasionally causes a sandy haze called the *calima*. A steady wind on the south coast creates ideal windsurfing conditions.

## Flora and fauna

These climatic conditions and the unusual geological features have nurtured a variety of plants and wildlife, some of which are unique to the island. Comparable with Hawaii, the Galapagos and other archipelagos that have their own biodiversity, the Canary Islands as a whole have around 650 native species and nearly 40 percent of the territory is under some sort of conservation order. On Tenerife, 400 of the 2,000 naturally occurring plant species are endemic.

Tenerife's extraordinary environment has attracted botanists down the centuries. From Germany came Alexander von Humboldt, who, in the 19th century, stopped on his way

Bird of paradise, the Canaries' flower and a major export

to South America and gave the islands fulsome praise. The French diplomat Sabin Berthelot, an enthusiast for all things Canarian, arrived on the island in 1820 at the age of 26 and became director of the botanical gardens. From England in 1875 came Marianne North, whose works fill the gallery named after her at Kew Gardens in London.

What they found were tree-sized poinsettias, local variants of laurel and euphorbia, the *Phoenix canariensis* palm and the legendary dragon tree *(Dracaena draco)*. Among many flowers that make the island particularly attractive in May and June are the red pillars of Teide echium or 'pride of Tenerife' *(orgullo di Tenerife)* and the pink-and-white Teide broom *(Spartocytisus nubigens)*, both of which thrive in the arid Cañadas.

The island has thousands of insect species, though none is likely to do you any harm. There are grasshoppers native to each island, and the ones on Tenerife grow to 12cm (5in). Its reptiles include the Canary species of lizard, skink and gecko.

## Bird life

Many of the birds found on Tenerife will be familiar to Europeans, but there are different ones to look out for, too. Most are shy, however, and stay out of the sun, and though a variety of coloured doves are evident, don't expect to see many species as you travel around. The blue Teide finch, for example, might be seen in the National Park. Forests of Canarian pines are home to the blue chaffinch (endangered after the fires of July 2007 wiped out much of the island's pine forests) and the canary, a dull bird in the wild, which becomes yellow and more boisterous when caged (or blinded, as they once were to make them sing louder). In the scrubland you might see the Canarian pipit, Barbary partridge or Trumpeter finch. In the laurel and juniper forests, look out for the Canary Island kinglet and native pigeons. Other unusual species include the collared pratincole, American golden plover, glossy ibis and Barbary falcon.

Harnessing the trade winds

You will see ocean birds around the headlands or if you go whale- or dolphin-watching. The Canaries are on one of the principal migration routes for whales: one third of all species pass through Canarian waters each year.

## Ecology

The island's habitat is continually under pressure, particularly from the four million or so tourists who arrive each year, making heavy demands on local resources. Tree felling, which began after the European conquest, has divested the island of lakes and rivers, and water is a precious commodity. Visitors should not be profligate with it. In addition, water treatment means that the taste might not always be great, so buying bottled water is both ecologically defensible and practical here.

Ecology is on the mind of every islander, as ranks of new cement-block villas and apartments continue to spread over the landscape. Summer forest fires, too, have disastrous effects,

Traditional dress

often started by tourists' lack of care. Environmental protection groups are active in a place where nature is the driving cultural force.

In 2007, severe forest fires burnt more than a third of Tenerife's forests and destroyed 900 homes. The Buenavista area and the Teno National Park were the worst affected. More recently, in 2012, fires near Teide volcano destroyed large swaths of forest in the Santa Cruz province.

## Population

The resident population, including 126,000 expatriates, is around 900,000, with more than half living in the conurbation of Santa Cruz. In the southern resorts where most visitors go, you are likely to encounter *godos* from Galicia and other poorer regions of the Spanish mainland, who come here to find work. *Tinerfeños* are cheerful, gregarious and courteous, with a love of children, parties and football. According to a folk song, 'Canarians are like the giant Teide, quiet as snow on the outside and fire in the heart'. Their carnival is, after all, one of the greatest in the world. No trace of the tall, fair-haired Guanche survives, though DNA sampling, using Guanche mummies (see page 16), shows traces in a percentage of islanders.

The local Spanish accent is halfway between Madrid and Mexico. The 'c' and 'z' are not a lisped *th* as they are on the mainland, and consonants at the end of words sometimes fall away (examples include Santa Cru', La' Palma', and Juá instead of Juan). Some words come directly from South America (*guagua* for a bus), others from the colonial past – *chóni* for a foreigner, from the English 'Johnny' foreigner.

## Economy

Tourism is the main occupation of the islanders today. Agriculture is on the wane and some of the more remote villages have become abandoned. Since the conquest the island has had a series of monocultures, from sugar to bananas and cochineal. Bananas are still one of the main crops grown, along with tomatoes and cut flowers, particularly the bird of paradise flower *(strelitzia)*. Wine-making is limited to domestic consumption.

There are no mineral resources on the island, and no industry. As produce and manufactured goods have to be shipped in, the cost of living tends to be higher than in mainland Spain.

## Government

The Canary Islands are one of the autonomous regions of Spain and a member of the European Union. Santa Cruz de Tenerife is the administrative capital of the western islands and Las Palmas on Gran Canaria the capital of the eastern islands. The presidency, which coincides with local elections, rotates between the two capitals every four years. The 60-member parliament meets in the parliament building in Santa Cruz, while the Supreme Court sits in Las Palmas.

### Isle of dogs

The native island dog is the Verdino. Smooth-haired and powerful, it weighs 40–50kg (90–110lb) and gets its name from its colour, which is slightly greenish. There is a theory that the islands were named after the native dogs (*canes* in Latin) found here in classical times.

# A BRIEF HISTORY

La Orotava Valley behind Puerto de la Cruz on the north coast of Tenerife is the most fertile and pleasant part of the island. When the island's Hispanic conquerors arrived in the 15th century they found the Taoro living here, the richest of nine island tribes, whose chief or *mencey* was called Tanasú. These tall, fair-skinned, blue-eyed people called Guanches somehow reached the Canary Islands in the 1st or 2nd century BC from northwest Africa, and were related to Berbers. They developed a written language, which remains largely undeciphered, and were ruled through councils called *tagorors*, with their court in Adeje on the west coast.

The island provided natural shelter with many caves (still used today in Chinameda and Fasnia), which they decorated; they built stone huts, too.

## Guanche culture

Not surprisingly, the volcanic giant of El Teide was central to worship for the Guanches. Their culture can be glimpsed through their funerary rites and in particular their mummifying rituals, which are explained at the Museo de la Naturaleza y el Hombre in Santa Cruz. They probably worshipped the sun, and the ancient 'pyramids' that the Norwegian explorer Thor Heyerdahl revealed in 1990 in Güímar are convincing evidence of how their ritual buildings may have looked.

The Guanches built no boats, nor did the wheel occur to them, but they were adept potters, making

### Mysterious journey

The Guanches were, it is supposed, related to the Berbers, but how they reached the Canary Islands from Africa is a mystery. The Romans arrived to find that the islanders did not possess boats.

Moss furring an ancient pot

their finest vessels for religious purposes and storing grain. Pottery and cultivation was women's work. Men hunted and tended the animals. A lack of metal ore on the island left the Guanches stuck in the stone age, with blunt instruments sharpened by bones and black volcanic obsidian, found in the Cañadas.

For food, they hunted wild cats and pigs, Barbary partridges and quail. They also kept pigs, sheep and, principally, goats, whose skins provided the material of the 'loose cassocks' that they wore. But it was as a land of dogs that the island group may have been given its name. In the 1st century ad Pliny wrote of an expedition to the islands by King Juba II of Mauretania, who apparently saw many dogs roaming there. *Canis* is the Latin for dog, hence Canary Islands. The islands were fixed on the earliest classical maps as the *'Insulae Fortunatae'*, the Fortunate Islands, and were the furthest western point of the known world.

## The conquest

Spanish cartographers properly mapped the islands at the end of the 14th century when the name Tenerife (actually 'Tenerifiz') appeared for the first time. The Genoese Lanzarotto Malocello is generally thought to have led the first European expedition to the Canaries, landing in the 1330s on the island that bears his name. Within a few decades, conquest of the islands had begun. Jean de Béthencourt, a Norman adventurer employed by Henri III of Castile, made the initial advances, capturing the eastern isles and then, in 1405, El Hierro, the smallest of the western isles. Tenerife, the most populous of the islands, was still in Guanche hands in 1492 when Christopher Columbus stopped at neighbouring Gran Canaria and La Gomera on his way to the New World (noting, as he did so, an eruption of El Teide, and recording that his crew thought it a sign that they should turn back).

## Missionaries and conquerors

That same year, Alfonso Fernandez de Lugo, a mercenary backed by Genoese merchants, seized La Palma, following a six-year campaign against Gran Canaria. Only Tenerife remained in native hands. The influence of the conquerors of the other islands had spread to Tenerife and de Lugo's way was paved by the missionary activities of a local woman convert and lay preacher, Francisca de Gazmira. On the coast de Lugo easily defeated local tribes, moving to the better defended interior where he

In the Laboratory of Natural History

tricked the chief Tanasú of the Taoro tribe with a sham parley. Finally, however, he was caught in a trap at Barranco de Acentejo (now the town of La Matanza, 'the slaughter') 16km (10 miles) into the Orotava Valley.

De Lugo escaped, only to return to the island with a larger force the following year and win a decisive victory on the plains of La Vitoria de Acentejo, a couple of miles south of his earlier defeat. Some 2,000 Guanches were cut down by the sophisticated Spanish crossbow, and Tanasú, the last chief of the Taoro, committed suicide.

Statue of a Guanche King in Candelaria

De Lugo established his capital at San Cristóbal de la Laguna in the middle of the fertile Valle de Aguere, within striking distance of both the north and east coasts. The statue of Jesus that he had brought to the island came to rest here in the Santuario del Cristo, and the flag that had claimed Tenerife for Spain was subsequently hung in the town hall. Santa Iglesia cathedral, which was founded ten years later in 1515, became de Lugo's resting place.

The effect of the conquerors on the local population was disastrous. The new diseases they brought spread among the Guanche population and many were taken into slavery, though the nobles were accorded due respect, and some of them intermarried. From the thousands that had inhabited the island, soon only a few hundred remained. The investors in de Lugo's expedition were rewarded with plots of land in the west, where sugar cane was introduced for the refineries built at Realejos, Duate and Icod. De Lugo continued to seek Italian finance to fuel the new economy and Portuguese workers were imported to harvest the canes on a share-cropping basis.

## Sugar and wine

The landscape began to change, too. Mills were stoked with timber cut from the forests, which had the long-term effect of reducing rainfall and drying up lakes, streams and springs.

Canarian sugar could not compete with that being planted in the New World, so by the end of the 15th century vineyards of the Malvasía grape had been established on the east of the island instead, and it was wine that offered an alternative economy as the sugar trade slumped. The grape produced sweet, dessert wines that travelled well and were particularly enjoyed by northern Europeans. By the time Shakespeare's Falstaff and Sir Toby Belch were downing 'cups of Canary', and Bostonians were talking of 'the Isles of Wine', it had become the principal export.

The Canary Islands benefited from being on the trade route to the New World, and ships regularly visited Tenerife's excellent harbours, principally Garachico on the north coast, carrying sugar and slaves. Trade between Spain and the New World was confined to Spanish nationals, so smuggling and piracy became part of daily life. But in 1610 the Spanish government relaxed this restriction and foreign capitalists headed for Tenerife. By the mid-century, the island had 1,500 English and Dutch residents out of a population of 50,000.

The Malvasía grape's rival was Madeira, from the Portuguese island of the same name, and when England sided with Portugal in the War of the Spanish Succession (1701–14) a major market was lost. However, Tenerife remained the islands' major wine producer for another century, and the wealth that it brought paid for the rich architecture of wine towns such as Orotava. In 1706, when a volcanic eruption devastated Garachico, Puerto de la Cruz became the island's main port.

A university was founded in La Laguna at the start of the 18th century and an intelligentsia flourished among the 70,000 *tinerfeños*. But prosperity did not survive the century and the wine trade diminished. Global conflict, with America's War of Independence and the Napoleonic wars, during which Admiral Nelson blockaded Santa Cruz, was harmful to trade. Hardship was compounded by revolutions in Latin America, where many Canarians had gone to seek their fortunes, and

Admiral Nelson, wounded at Tenerife in 1797

payments to the families left behind were disrupted. The Canaries themselves were not without revolutionary fervour, and in 1819 the local junta put forward the islanders' desire to 'get rid of all the Spaniards now here and to put the people of this land in their place'.

## Beetles to bananas

After the wine trade slumped, the cochineal beetle was introduced from Mexico, mainly in the eastern isles. This had a brutalising effect on the landscape as native trees were replaced by cactus for the beetle to feed on. The crop went into decline when synthetic dyes were introduced in the late 19th century, by which time bananas, said to have been introduced by the French consul, Sabin Berthelot, were making money.

In 1822 Santa Cruz had become the official capital of the archipelago and 30 years later each island was granted free trade status

An early 20th century image of a Dracona tree

for one of its ports, though Tenerife had two: Puerto de la Cruz and Santa Cruz, which then had the archipelago's only first-class road, to La Orotava. Tenerife's superiority took a knock in 1881, though, when a harbour improvement scheme for Las Palmas on Gran Canaria eclipsed Santa Cruz.

### Independence

Secundino Delgado was the most influential independence figure. He went to work in Cuba at 14, but it was in Venezuela, in 1897, that he founded *El Guanche*, a newspaper calling for independence in the Canary Islands.

A profound change began at the end of the 19th century, when refrigeration arrived and tourists came too, on the fruit boats. The Grand Hotel Taoro in Puerto de la Cruz was built in 1892 to cater for them, and for many years it was the largest hotel in Spain.

## The Spanish Civil War

The Spanish Second Republic of 1931 brought new hopes of autonomy but General Franco's uprising of 1936 put paid to any such aspirations for more than 40 years. Suspected of plans against the Republican government, Franco had been sent to Tenerife in March to put him out of the way. From Las Palmas, however, he flew to the Spanish North African enclave of Melilla on 18 July. Two days later the uprising that led to the civil war was underway and the islands were in Franco's hands – La Palma was shelled by the navy before being overcome. On Tenerife, Lt Gonzales Campos was the only officer to oppose the uprising and he was shot, along with the civil governor. Republican prisoners and suspects were herded into Fyffes' banana warehouse, near Santa Cruz football ground, and shot in batches. An ally of Hitler and Mussolini, Franco was ostracised by the rest of the world until the early 1950s when Spain was welcomed back into the international community in exchange for accepting Nato bases.

## Tourism and the post-Franco years

After Franco's death in 1975, King Juan Carlos restored democracy. Three years later a new Constitution granted degrees of autonomy to the country's regions, including the Canary Islands.

Tourism had already begun with a vengeance in Tenerife, after direct flights to the island started in 1959. Pressure on Puerto de la Cruz to build more hotels caused people within the area to sell up and transfer their plantations to the dry south, piping water into the region and opening up the barren lands in Adeje and Arona. On this coast, tourists in search of a tan flocked to the port of Los Cristianos. This is where the boom really happened, sprawling up into Playa de las Américas, which was created in 1978, the same year that the nearby airport of Reina Sofia opened. Resorts still continue to spread along the coast, boosting the island's economy.

Today, the majority of tourists head for these resorts, which are renowned for cheap package breaks and non-stop nightlife. However, an increasing number of visitors are discovering the greener, quieter and more traditional Tenerife of the north.

Tourism is the new monoculture

New hotels here, many in rustic or local Canarian style, are luring visitors who want to get off the beaten track. On the island as a whole, new or refurbished luxury and boutique hotels, year-round golf, chic nightlife, whale-watching, great trekking and the opening of gourmet restaurants are successfully working to change the long-held image of a downmarket 'sun, sea and sand' destination.

# Historical landmarks

**c. 3000BC** Settlers arrive from Africa.

**206BC** Guanches reach the island.

**1st century AD** Classical writers describe the islands on the edge of the known world populated by dogs (*canis*, hence Canaries).

**1st–13th centuries** Guanche society develops under tribal chiefs.

**1440s** Jean de Béthencourt, a Norman adventurer, captures the island of Hierro but fails to take Tenerife.

**1492** Christopher Columbus witnesses eruption of Mt Teide en route to discovering the Americas.

**1495** Tanasú, the last chief of the Taoro, commits suicide when Tenerife is conquered by Alfonso Fernandez de Lugo at the Battle of Acentejo.

**1656** Sixteen Spanish galleons bringing gold from the Americas are sunk in Santa Cruz harbour by the British under Admiral Blake.

**1701–14** The Canaries' university founded in La Laguna.

**1706** Mount Teide erupts, destroying the main port of Garachico.

**1797** Admiral Nelson's attack on Santa Cruz repelled.

**1850–1900** Large scale emigration to Latin America.

**1880s** Bananas introduced.

**1936** General Franco launches his rebellion from Tenerife.

**1959** First direct flights to Tenerife bring a new wave of tourists.

**1978** The Canaries become autonomous within Spain.

**1986** Spain joins the European Union and negotiates a special status for the Canaries.

**1995** Canary Islands integrated into the EU but retain important tax privileges.

**1999** The euro replaces the peseta as the currency of Spain.

**2006** Sharp rise in the number of illegal immigrants from Africa.

**2007** Severe forest fires strike the west of the island.

**2010** Teide National Park provides a backdrop for the new film version of *Clash of the Titans* and two years later for its sequel *Wrath of the Titans*.

**2012** Fires destroy large swathes of forest in the Santa Cruz province.

**2015** Municipal elections in Tenerife.

# WHERE TO GO

Tenerife is not large and as a result, it is easy to make forays from any base. Nowhere is far away, as cruise-ship passengers discover when, docking in Santa Cruz with just four hours ashore, they find they have enough time for a coach to take them to the top of El Teide and back, stopping off at La Orotava for some souvenirs, or even to hire a car and make their own way to the cable car to reach the summit.

For much of the island, however, you don't need a car. Buses are regular and inexpensive. From the capital, Santa Cruz, you can have a day out on the opposite coast in Puerto de la Cruz, the north coast resort, stopping off at the unesco World Heritage Site of San Cristóbal de La Laguna, with enough time to enjoy both places at leisure and return later in the day. You can also make day trips to these places from Los Cristianos and Playa de las Américas in the south. A hire car of course adds convenience and allows you to stop to photograph a view, inspect the flowers, or take advantage of signs of honey or wine for sale.

The descriptions that follow start in Santa Cruz and continue anti-clockwise around the island.

## THE NORTHEAST

### Santa Cruz de Tenerife

Tenerife's capital, principal port and most vibrant town is on the northeastern arm of the island, facing southwest and looking towards Gran Canaria, its rival, an hour's jet-foil ferry trip away. **Santa Cruz de Tenerife ❶** doesn't have a real heart, a

Playa de las Teresitas, with Santa Cruz in the distance

The Cabildo Insular and post office on Plaza de España

municipal or cathedral square; instead the main action takes place on the pedestrianised streets and squares leading up from the port, and on the Rambla that sweeps round the top of the town. Good for shops, restaurants and nightlife, Santa Cruz is also the cultural hub of Tenerife.

The extensive waterfront area reaches its apex at **Plaza de España ⓐ**; to the southwest are the container ports and the industrial zone, to the northeast the jacaranda-lined Avenida de Anaga passes beside the ferry port and yachting harbour. The square has undergone a complete transformation by the innovative Swiss architects Herzog and de Meuron. The new focal point is a huge circular wading pool with a geyser-like fountain in the centre, accompanied by newly planted trees. The former heart of the square, the **Monumento a los Caídos**, dedicated to the fallen Nationalists in the Civil War, has been integrated into the new design.

The Art Deco buildings at the southern end of the square are the post office headquarters and the **Cabildo Insular**, containing government offices and the main tourist office.

*Shopping area*

Running up from the Plaza de España is **Plaza Candelaria**, where a statue of the island's patron dates from 1772. This is the start of the main pedestrianised area and the pavement cafés are a popular meeting place. **Calle del Castillo ❸**, the principal shopping street, heads inland past the **Parlamento de Canarias** (tours, also guided, every Sat), on the right. The 1898 neoclassical building, designed by Antonio Pintor, has been augmented to include the buildings fronting Castillo, with a green metal construction on its upper floors. Calle del Castillo ends at **Plaza del General Weyler**, where the white marble *La Fuente* (*The Fountain*) by Achille Canessa is overlooked by the Capitanía General, the islands' military headquarters. This is where Franco was stationed when he started the Civil War. There's a café in the southwest corner where you can sit and watch the world go by.

On the north side of Calle del Castillo is the **Plaza del Principe**, one of the town's most pleasant squares. On the square's southeast side, near the Circulo de Amistad, is the **Museo Municipal de Bellas Artes ❹** (Tue–Fri 10am–8pm, Sat–Sun 10am–3pm; free). The front of the building has busts of poets, philosophers and musicians. Inside is a library and, on the first and second floors, a gallery of 16th- to 20th-century paintings. These include a panoramic picture of the foundation of Santa Cruz by Alonso de Lugo in 1494, two years after he had taken the island, and among portraits of local aristocracy is one of

**Record carnival**

Santa Cruz entered the *Guinness World Records* when a record crowd of a quarter of a million filled the Plaza de España for the 1987 carnival. The Tenerife carnival is one of the biggest in Europe.

the French consul and botanist Sabin Berthelot, who did so much for the island's plant life.

Behind the museum is the **Iglesia de San Francisco**, founded in 1680 and part of a former convent where concerts sometimes take place.

### The oldest church

Eight years after Santa Cruz was founded, the town's first chapel was built where the city's main church, **Nuestra Señora de la Concepción ❶**, stands today, just to the southwest of the Cabildo Insular. The cross that de Lugo brought ashore is among its treasures. In 1652 the church was rebuilt after a fire, its octagonal tower acting as a look-out point. The lovely balcony on its exterior, a feature of church architecture throughout the island, gives its southwest front a domestic appearance. Inside, the space is cool and impressive and the beautiful coffered *mudéjar*-style ceiling is also typical of the island.

In the streets around the church are some of the oldest buildings in Santa Cruz and they have been attractively maintained in warm earth colours. Stop for a drink in J.C. Murphy's in the little church square. This area comes alive at night, with busy cafés and bars open until the early hours. Where Calle Dominguez Alfonso meets Puente General Serrador there is a small square where evening concerts are held.

If you are strolling here in the evening, you may be lucky to chance on street theatre where the actors use the doors and balconies of the houses in their performances. Nearby is the **Teatro Guimerá** (www.

La Concepción

Teatro Guimerá

teatroguimera.es), named after the playwright Ángel Guimerá, who was born in Santa Cruz in 1849, and made his name in Barcelona with *Terra Baixa* in 1896. It also features concerts and dance performances. Not far, on Calle Clavel 10, is yet another cultural centre – El Generador (www.equipopara.org) – a meeting place for artists and intellectuals as well as a concert, workshop and exhibition venue with the benefit of a small bar.

## Across the Barranco

From Nuestra Señora de la Concepción a bridge crosses a *barranco* (dry river bed) to the former town hospital, now the **Museo de la Naturaleza y el Hombre E** (Tue–Sat 9am–8pm, Sun–Mon 10am–5pm;www.museosdetenerife.org). As the name implies, all island life is here, and this is a good starting point for understanding Tenerife's geographical and historical aspects. Set out on three floors around two courtyards, it swarms with schoolchildren in term-time, but is large enough to allow you to browse in peace. The island's flora and fauna are fully explained, as is its geology, with descriptions of winds, currents and volcanoes. Man features early on, with mummified Guanches, and displays show how the indigenous population lived. At the end is a café and an excellent bookshop.

Just west of the museum is the **Tenerife Espacio de las Artes** (tea; www.teatenerife.es) designed by Swiss architects duo Herzog and de Meuron. This huge new multi-functional exhibition centre, along with the auditorium has given the city a cultural focus. It houses numerous exhibition halls, Tenerife Island Photography Centre and a splendid library. Nearby on Plaza de Santa Cruz de la Sierra is the **Mercado de Nuestra Señora de África** ❼, popularly known as **La Recova** (www.la-recova.com). This vibrant morning market shows the bounty of the island piled high, with its range of flowers, aromatic herbs, fruit, vegetables, meat and fish spread across two floors. On Sunday mornings there is a flea market, and stalls extend down Calle José Manuel Guimerá.

### Auditorio and Parque Marítimo

Calle José Manuel Guimerá leads down to the main highway, Avenida del Tres de Mayo, which connects the docks to the Autopista del Norte, while the Avenida de la Constitución continues past the port towards the Autopista del Sur. The latter has

## Gentlemen at war

In 1797 Admiral Nelson attacked Santa Cruz. Leading the night assault, he leapt ashore only to have his right elbow shattered by grapeshot from a cannon in the Castillo de Paso Alto. The assault was a failure but the Spanish Governor sent each captured man back to his ship with a bottle of wine and a loaf of bread. His arm amputated, Nelson returned the compliment by sending the governor cheese and a cask of beer. The captured British flags are stored in a glass case in Nuestra Señora de le Concepción church.

The Auditorio, home of the Tenerife Symphony Orchestra

become the focus of post-millennium developments with the elegant **Auditorio de Tenerife Adán Martín** or **Auditorio** (guided tours Mon–Sat at 12.30pm, www.auditoriodetenerife.com), a concert hall built in 2003 by Valencian architect Santiago Calatrava. It is home to the Tenerife Symphony Orchestra. Beside it is a bus station, and behind it, beyond the old **Castillo San Juan**, is the **Parque Marítimo César Manrique** Ⓖ (Avenida Constitución 5; daily 10am–6pm). The park is a breezy area of azure seawater pools designed by the Lanzarote artist César Manrique (see page 46), with trees, flowers and waterfalls. With a cafeteria and restaurant, a day out here is as good as at the beach. Beside it is a **Palmetum** (daily 10am–6pm; till 5 pm in winter; http://palmetumtenerife.es) with palm trees from all over the world.

## The Rambla

Santa Cruz's other main avenue, the **Rambla**, meanders around the back of the town and arrives at the Avenida de Anaga, by the waterfront next to the **Museo Militar Regional de Canarias** (Tue–Sat 10am–2pm; free). This contains some of the armour worn by the Spanish conquerors, souvenirs from Nelson's attack, including El Tigre, the cannon that shattered his right elbow (see box), and the background to Franco's uprising in 1936. The Rambla's central pedestrian walkway, under jacaranda and Judas trees, makes it ideal for the evening *paseo* (stroll). Outdoor sculpture exhibitions have been held here since the 1970s and Henry Moore's *Goslar Warrior* is among a number of works that remain. To add to the pleasures of the Rambla, there are Chinese, Lebanese and Italian restaurants, the Cine Victor cinema and the bull ring, used mainly for pop concerts. The Rambla also passes the town's largest park, the 6-hectare (15-acre) **Parque García Sanabria** Ⓗ, which has exotic plants and a pleasant café. A Swiss-made *Reloj de Flores* (Flower Clock), situated by the entrance near Calle Pilar, is one of *Santacruceros'* favourite meeting points.

### The city's beach

Avenida de Anaga continues north, following the coast past the yacht clubs from where tycoon Robert Maxwell set sail for the last time in 1991, then towards the town's playground, **Playa de las Teresitas** ➋ (served by the No. 910 bus, which runs the 7km/4 miles along the waterfront every 10–20 minutes). It is the most golden beach on the island, its imported Sahara sand lapped by shallow waters. Dogs, surfboards, ball games and the hanging of towels or clothes on trees are all banned. Kiosks sell snacks, and at weekends locals

Picturesque Igueste

Playa de las Teresitas

enliven the atmosphere at the restaurants, notably the Cofradía de Pescadores by the fishermen's shacks. There are more places to eat in **San Andrés** ❸, the fishing village of the original port just outside Santa Cruz, where the road heads into the Anaga Hills. After 15 minutes' drive the road reaches the **Mirador de Rosa Sosa**, offering a last, stunning glimpse of the coast as well as walks through glorious, herb-scented hills.

On the coast beyond Playa de las Teresitas the road winds without let-up, with the exception of the **Punta de los Organos** *mirador*, which provides a last chance to look down on the beach. A couple of kilometres further on, a turn leads down to the secluded beach of Las Gaviotas beneath the cliffs, where swimsuits are optional. The road ends at **Igueste**, an attractive cluster of white villas among terraces of mangoes and avocados, winding steeply down before coming to a stop several hundred metres short of a small grey beach. From here you can walk to the little beach and one-family hamlet of

**Antequera**. The Rincon de Anaga is a family-run restaurant at the entrance to Igueste.

## San Cristóbal La Laguna

Designated the capital of Tenerife by the island's conqueror, Alonso de Lugo, **San Cristóbal de la Laguna** ❹ is visibly the most ancient town on the island, with mansions dating from the 15th century. It is generally known simply as La Laguna, but the lagoon on which it was once sited and named for has long since disappeared. The town, a World Heritage Site, is at the centre of a large agricultural district, and is a centre of learning and religion, with a university and bishop's see.

Just inland from Santa Cruz, La Laguna is regarded as a suburb of the capital, but in the 20 minutes or so that it takes to reach it, the climate can noticeably cool, and you should take warmer clothing. The old part of town, the *casco histórico*, is on a grid system, and the starting point of a visit should be the **Plaza del Adelantado**. The municipal market once held at the far end of the square has been temporarily rehoused on La Plaza del Cristo, 10 minutes' walk away. The town is popular with visitors from the capital on weekends, when parking is difficult and the square's bars are buzzing. On the opposite side of the square are a trio of impressive but disparate buildings. To the left is the neoclassical **Ayuntamiento** (town hall), which contains the flag that de Lugo planted when he arrived from Spain. (The nearby tourist office offers a free plan as well as one-hour walking tours of the old town). To the right is the **Palacio de Nava**, a baroque mansion that belonged to the Marquis de Villanueva del Prado in the early 18th century, whose glittering salon attracted the thinkers of the day. He was also responsible for establishing the Botanic Garden in La

### Taking the tram

A tram service linking La Laguna with Santa Cruz offers splendid views. See www.tranviatenerife.com for timetables and prices.

Intricately carved balcony, La Laguna

Orotava. In between is the massive **Iglesia-Convento de Santa Catalina de Siena**, with a 'Canarian' balcony on the corner from where the nuns can glimpse the outside world.

Calle Obispo Rey Redondo leads along the blank wall of the convent, past three 17thcentury mansions which make this the most impressive corner of town. The tourist office is housed in the Casa de Alvarado Bracamonte (daily 9am–5pm, until 3pm on Sat–Sun). Wander down this street to the **Catedral**, where de Lugo is buried behind the altar, and the **Iglesia de la Concepción** (Tue–Sat 10am–noon and 5–7.30pm, Sun 8.30am–noon and 5.30–7.15pm), which dates from 1502. Its font was used to baptise converted Guanche leaders. In Calle San Agustin, at No 22, it is possible to see the interior of a mansion, Casa Lercaro, home to a branch of **Museo de Historia y Antropología de Tenerife** (MHAT, Tue–Sat 9am–8pm, Sun–Mon 10am–5pm; free Fri–Sat 4–8pm; www.museosdetenerife. org). This fine building, with its own small chapel, was built by

Typical Romeria fiesta party in Los Abrigos

the Genoan Lercaro family of bankers in 1593, the owner's first son, Francisco, becoming the Lt-Governor of Tenerife. Nearby, located at San Agustin No 18 in a beautifully restored historic *casona* (house) is **Fundación Crisitino de Vera** (www.fundacioncristinode vera.org) featuring a collection of paintings by the contemporary Canarian artist Cristino de Vera Reyes.

From the Plaza del Adelantado, Calle Nava de Grimón leads past the peach-coloured walls of the **Convento de Santa Clara de Asis** (Mon–Sat 7–11.45am, Sun 6.30–8pm; only patio), the town's other immense convent housing the Sacred Art Museum (Calle Viana 38, Tue, Thu, Sat 10am–5pm), which tells its history and displays valuable works including 18th and 19th century paintings, to the Convent of San Miguel de las Victorias Franciscanes. Here, the **Santuario del Santísimo Cristo de La Laguna** contains a figure of Christ commissioned by de Lugo from a Flemish sculptor in 1520. Dripping with New World silver and gold, it is the town's most venerated figure.

Two major museums are within reach of La Laguna. On the outskirts of the town is the **Museo de la Ciencia y el Cosmos** (Avda. Los Mencelles 70; Tue–Sat 9am–8pm; Mon–Sun 10am–5pm; free Fri–Sat 4–8pm; www.museosdetenerife.org). This hands-on museum is an introduction to cosmology and the planets. The other is yet another branch of the excellent **Museo de Historia y Antropología de Tenerife** in the Casa de Carta in Valle de Guerra (Vino 44; daily 10am–5pm; free Fri–Sat 1–5pm). This museum of popular culture is beautifully laid out, and depicts five centuries of rural life on the island.

The fertile Valle de Guerra is a centre for flower growing. Looking down on it is the **Mirador de El Boquerón**, where a map shows the distribution of agriculture; the main crops are bananas, avocados, potatoes, vines and the bird of paradise flower, which has become a symbol of the islands.

To the east, beyond the villages of **Tegueste** and **Tejina**, is **Bajamar ❺**, a small, old-fashioned resort where people from La Laguna come to soak in the sea-water pools. Beyond it is **Punto Hidalgo**, a good place for coastal walks, which are signposted from the roundabout at the end of the town. The flower-covered Café Melita on the way into Punto Hidalgo has wonderful cakes and pastries, plus views over the sea.

Taganana is a distinctive community

## The Anaga Hills

The best view of La Laguna is from the **Mirador Jardín** in the **Monte de las Mercedes**. Looking down on the town and both coasts, it has a helpful explanation of where the lagoon was and how it gradually faded away. Listen for canaries in the trees and bushes. You might glimpse one, but they are not as brightly coloured in the wild as they are in captivity.

Las Mercedes forest is the start of the **Montañas de Anaga**, a series of volcanic hills rising to about 1,000m (3,300ft) with deep valleys running down to the sea, ending in small beaches accessible only by boat or after hours of walking. The best place to begin is beyond the Jardín at a **second mirador, Cruz del Carmen** at 920m (3,018ft), though the thickets of heather and fern give less of a view. The visitor centre (daily 9.00am–4pm) for the **Parque Rural Anaga** is here. There is a small exhibition about the natural history of the local area, and an information point can suggest walks. Just beyond Cruz del Carmen a turning to the right leads to the **Mirador del Pico del Inglés**, one of the best viewpoints on the island. After El Bailadero, beneath which the north–south road tunnels, it becomes little more than a single track wandering all the way to **Chamorga**, a one-bar community at the end of the road.

The road north of El Bailadero leads through **Taganana**, a community of white houses and palms, which in 1881 felt so cut off it declared itself independent. Its 15th-century church is one of the oldest on the island. Beyond it is **Playa San Roque**, where surfers gather on the small beach in front of the buzzy Bar Playa Casa Africa. Further on is a string of restaurants at **Roques de las Bodegas**, and at **Benijo** the road dissolves into paths heading over the cliffs.

## Walking in the Anaga Hills

Walking is the best way to explore the Anaga Hills. A starting point is the Visitor Centre at Cruz del Carmen, or the Albergue Montes de Anaga (www.alberguestenerife.net; see page 134), where you can obtain maps of the *senderos* (paths). Several walks begin around Las Carboneras, including one down to the sea at Punto Hidalgo, passing through three identifiable ecosystems. A more dramatic walk is from Chamorga at the end of the road down to Faro de Anaga, the lighthouse on the northeastern tip.

View of the city Puerto de la Cruz

The dense vegetation of these hills includes the largest natural laurel forest in the Canary Islands, their leaves often dripping with moisture from the misty climate produced by the trade winds. Their prehistoric ecosystem supports bay trees, holly, heather and spurge, while the damp climate keeps alive the ferns, lichen and moss. There are also a number of cave houses here, such as those at **Chinamada**, where one of them has been turned into a bar and restaurant called La Cueva.

## THE NORTH COAST

The fertile Orotava Valley made the Guanche tribe here the wealthiest on the island. It did the same for the colonisers who made the most of the ideal growing conditions, building impressive mansions on the proceeds. Villa Orotava, as La Orotava was then called, was a gateway up to El Teide. Just below it, where the valley arrived at the sea, was Puerto de la Orotava,

Playa Jardín, Puerto de la Cruz

a handy port from where wine and other products could be shipped abroad. However, in 1706 a volcanic eruption destroyed the north coast's major port of Garachico. Overnight Puerto de la Orotava's fortunes increased, and the port was renamed Puerto de la Cruz as a sign that it would do business with the whole island. When tourism started, this part of the island was where the curious visitors came, for the climate, the Botanic Gardens, the architecture and for El Teide. By then Alexander Humboldt had paid a visit and made his pronouncements. A *mirador* between La Orotava and Puerto de la Cruz marks the spot where the German naturalist expressed his delight in the view, though he was not so delighted when he returned from his trip up El Teide to discover that his porters had abandoned the plant and mineral samples he had collected, because they thought them unnecessary ballast. It was not long before other botanists and natural philosophers were making the journey up the mountain, followed by the first holidaymakers. When the Grand Hotel Taoro was built in Puerto de la Cruz in 1892 it was the largest in Spain.

## Puerto de la Cruz

One of the pioneering resorts of Spain, and the oldest in Tenerife, **Puerto de la Cruz** ❻ is a mix of high-rise blocks and, in the centre, handsome old buildings. Gently lit at night, the promenade wanders beneath palm trees and beside black rocks and beaches where white-crested waves pound. From the black beaches of Playa Jardín to Playa Martiánez, the seawater pools of Lago Martiánez and the small fishermen's quarter, it is a delight at any time of the day. The lively heart of the town is just inland from the harbour around the **Plaza del Charco de los Camarones**, named after a pool full of shrimps that was once here. There are café tables, kiosks, bands and the general hum of the town's life.

On the east side, Calle Quintana leads to the 16th-century **Ermita de San Juan Batista** and the 18th-century **Iglesia de San Francisco**, effectively one church with the dividing wall removed. They contain a medley of paintings of the Madonna.

The street continues up past two handsome mansions with elegant patios and balconies, now the hotels **Monopol** (www. monopoltf.com) and **Marquesa** (www.hotelmarquesa.com; see page 137). The Monopol, dating from 1742, was the birthplace of Agustín de Bethencourt y Molina, founder of the Madrid Civil Engineers' School and General Director of Ports and Roads for Alexander II of Russia. The Marquesa, more elegant still, has pavement tables perfect for people-watching. In front of them the street opens into the Plaza de la Iglesia and the town's principal church, **Iglesia de Nuestra Señora de la Peña de Francia**, built in 1697 with a tower added in 1898. The organ was made in London.

### The harbour

The harbour today is small with little activity, and it is hard to imagine it as a stopping point for transatlantic

> ## Plaza Galdós
>
> Plaza Pérez Galdós (also known as La Placeta), named after the Spanish playwright and novelist who was born in Gran Canaria in 1843, is the most pleasant square in La Ranilla. Stop here for a drink or *tapas* at one of the small restaurants or bars.

Dolphin at Loro Parque

trade. However, once the planned €92 million project consisting of a new marina, ferry terminal and fishing harbour – as well as maritime park – is completed in the next few years, the harbour area will be completely transformed. On the eastern side, the distinctive **Casa de la Aduana**, the former customs house and residence of the royal tax collector (Mon–Sat 10am–8pm; free), contains Puerto de la Cruz's main **tourist office,** while another part houses an artesanal craft shop. Upstairs the **Museo de Arte Contemporáneo Eduardo Westerdahl** (MACEW, Museum of Contemporary Art, Mon–Sat 10am–2pm, Fri also 5–7.30pm) holds an interesting collection of modern Spanish artists and is the town's main cultural centre. To the west is **La Ranilla**, the fishermen's quarter, where you'll find a small **Museo Aequeológico** (Archeological Museum, Tue–Sat 10am–1pm and 5–9pm, Sun 10am–1pm; www.arqueopc. com) on Calle El Lomo. It houses a collection of Guanche ceramics. At the far end of La Ranilla, beyond the football ground and municipal swimming pool, is the 17th-century Castillo San Felipe, a small fort used for exhibitions. It marks the start of the town's main black beach, **Playa Jardín**, which is attractively landscaped behind. At the far end of the beach is Punta Brava and **Loro Parque** Ⓐ (www.loroparque.com; daily 8.30am–4pm, last exit 6.45pm), one of the island's big attractions, with killer whales, dolphin and sea lion shows, a penguin habitat, an aquarium and what is claimed to be the largest collection of parrots in the world. The Katendra Treetops is a free flight aviary with over 100 bird species.

## The promenade

On the eastern side of the port, behind the customs house, is the **Plaza de Europa**, a fake castle with genuine cannons, built in 1992 on top of a very handy central car park. The streets behind the square are full of handsome 18th- and 19th-century mansions with fine doorways and balconies. These lead to the promenade beside the small, rocky San Telmo beach where pools have been cut in the rocks for swimmers. The little white **San Telmo chapel**, dedicated to the patron saint of seamen, was built in 1780 on the site of a coastal battery.

On the point of land beyond here is the enchanting **Lago Martiánez** Ⓑ (Jan–May and mid Sep–Dec daily 10am–6pm, June–mid-Sept till 7pm), one of the town's great attractions.

Lago Martiánez, designed by Canadian artist César Manrique

With palms, boulders and sky-blue swimming pools, this wonderful area compensates for the lack of really good natural swimming facilities in the town. It was designed by César Manrique (1919–92), the artist from Lanzarote who did so much to promote the islands' natural resources. It is easy to spend a whole day in the complex, which has a café and restaurant, and thanks to a casino you can spend the evening here too.

The promenade, where Africans braid hair and sell carvings, bags and other leather goods, opens up as it reaches **Playa Martiánez**, the town's other beach that looks towards the cliffs rising to the east.

At the back of the town is the **Jardín Botánico** Ⓒ (www.icia.es; Apr–Sep daily 9am–7pm, 6pm in winter), properly known as Jardín de Aclimatación de la Orotava. It started life in 1788 as a staging post between the New World and Europe, allowing tropical and sub-tropical plants to become used to cooler temperatures. The pamphlet that comes with your entry ticket gives a layout of the garden and its species. As a scientific institute, it is especially dedicated to the flora of the Canary Islands, with more than 30,000 specimens. (The **Parque Taoro**, a landscape of gardens and ponds, is also a botanic delight.)

Monstera leaf in the botanical gardens of Puerto de la Cruz

Just beyond the Botanic Garden is the **Ábaco Casa Museo** (Tue–Sun 10am–1pm; www.abacotenerife.com), a beautiful 18th-century country house reconstructed with period furniture and a bounteous kitchen. The cocktail and piano bar opens in the evenings.

View from Plaza de la Constitución, Orotava, towards the coast

## La Orotava

The historic centre of Tenerife's most attractive town is unsign-posted, and visitors by car may find themselves going round in circles before they make it to the top right-hand side of the town where the island's wealthy landowners and merchants built their mansions. **La Orotava** ❼ is high above sea level and its streets are steep. Follow the 'Parking San Agustín' signs. Once you arrive, however, sites are helpfully marked and a useful map is available at the tourist office.

The church of **San Agustín**, which belonged to a former monastery, has a beautiful wood ceiling and a handsome retable. It sits at one end of the Plaza de la Constitución, which is overlooked by **Liceo de Taoro**, a grand private club, now open for the public to look around, and the adjacent **Jardínes Marquesado de la Quinta Roja**, also known as Jardín Victoria. These formal gardens were laid out in the 19th century around the mausoleum of the Marquis – membership

Casa de los Balcones

of the Masons precluded him from a burial on consecrated ground. Wilder and more lush are the **Hijuelo del Botánico** gardens just beyond. Worth visiting, too, is the nearby **Museo de Cerámica** (Calle Leon 3; Mon–Sat 10am–6pm, Sun 10am–4pm) in Casa Tafuriaste, a studio and showroom with a collection of traditional Spanish ceramics.

Calle Carrera del Escultor Estévez runs along the bottom of Plaza de la Constitución and west past the town's tourist information office. This street then leads past the **Ayuntamiento** (town hall), an imposing neoclassical building which gives a clue as to how important La Orotava once was. The square in front of it is brilliantly decorated during Corpus Christi (see page 96) using different coloured earth, sand and volcanic cinders.

Beyond here, the buildings give a sense of the riches that once flowed through the town. At the top of this road is the island's most famous domestic building, the 17th-century **Casa de los Balcones** (www.casa-balcones.com; Mon–Sat 8.30am–7.30pm,

Sun 8.30am–1.30pm; admission fee only for the museum) which, as its name suggests, has superlative wood balconies. For many years it has been associated with the island's lace making, along with several other outlets on the island. Staff in traditional costume will show you the best of the island's wares. Otherwise you can explore the beautiful patio and, for a small fee, the period rooms upstairs, peopled with dummies in costume, including a granny sound asleep in her bed.

**Casa del Turista**, the mansion opposite Casa de los Balcones, is almost as grand, and is part of the same outlet for island ware and lace. A few metres further up on the right is the Hospital de la Santísima Trinidad. Inside the courtyard is the revolving drum on the main door via which abandoned babies would be left in the care of the hospital's nuns.

*Town church*

Below these old streets is the **Iglesia de Nuestra Señora de la Concepción**, La Orotava's main church, built in the 16th century and rebuilt after devastating earthquakes in 1705, retaining the original marble altar. Further down the hill is the **Museo de Artesanía Iberoamericana** (Mon–Fri 10am–5pm,), which has an intriguing collection of ceramics, baskets, instruments and furniture from all over Latin America.

Opposite is the 17th-century **Casa Torrehermosa** which sells a selection of crafts, supported by the local government. There are several good restaurants in and around La Orotava, such as Sabor Canario and Victoria, which offer further opportunities to check out the interiors of the town's picturesque mansions.

Northwest of La Orotava (exit 35 off the TF-5), **Pueblo**

> **A fertile land**
>
> 'Around Orotava is the finest, most fertile land in these islands, and even in the whole of Spain, because on it can be grown and bred anything you may desire.' – Fray Alonso de Espinosa (1594)

**Chico** (www.pueblochico.com; daily 10am–5pm,) is a small park displaying island buildings in miniature. A further diversion to the east is the **Granja Verde** (Trasera Camino del Torreón, nº2, http://lagranjaverde.es; daily 10am–11pm) thematic park with 15 animal breeds and over 200 types of crops as main attractions. There are also two restaurants serving typical Canarian food.

## The wine lands of Tacoronte

East of Puerto de la Cruz, above the motorway on a pleasant rural road, are the villages of **La Mantanza de Acentejo** and **La Victoria de Acentejo**, scenes of the decisive battles between the Guanche *mencey* (chief), Bencomo, and the Spaniard Alonso Fernandez de Lugo. Matanza (the slaughter) is where 1,200 Spaniards were caught in a trap on 31 May, 1494. Only 200 escaped, de Lugo among them. He returned with a larger force the following year to win a decisive victory a short distance away at La Vitoria de Acentejo on Christmas Day 1495. Some 2,000 Guanche were slaughtered. It is difficult to imagine such scenes of carnage in these quiet hills.

Acres of vineyards mark this region out as **Tacoronte-Acentejo**, the best of the island's five do wine regions (see page 104). Just beyond La Matanza,

Casa del Vino, El Sauzal

the road goes under the motorway to arrive at **Casa del Vino La Baranda** (House of Wine, www.casadelvinotenerife.com; Wed–Sat 10am–9pm, Sun 11am–6pm, Tue 10.30am–6.30pm), just before entering El Sauzal. This 17th-century estate is an attractive collection of buildings that includes a wine press and museum with detailed displays in Spanish

San Pedro church, El Sauzal

and English about viniculture on Tenerife. It is an impressive story, and the number of different bottles on display – *tinto*, *rosado* and *blanco* – may come as a surprise to anyone who has been searching for a selection of Canary wines on restaurant menus. The House of Wine has its own bar and restaurant and a room for sampling and buying wine. To further delight the palate, visit the **Casa de la Miel** (House of Honey; Tue–Sat 10am–10pm, Sun 11am–6pm), also on the La Baranda estate and run by the island council as a centre for extracting and bottling honey.

High above the rocky coast, best seen from La Garañona *mirador*, and set on a slope is **El Sauzal** ❽, where the square outside the town hall teeters down attractive steps beside a waterfall. **Tacoronte**, too, is situated way above the sea and has a number of *bodegas* and restaurants. Its historic main square, Plaza del Cristo, is overlooked by a 17th-century church and convent of the same name; during Corpus Christi, coloured earth and flowers carpet the square. Ten minutes' walk down a steep hill is the church of **Santa Catalina**, with a typical balcony. It has two of the finest retables on the island and among its paintings is a fine *Inmaculada* by José Luján Pérez. The coast at Tacoronte looks tantalisingly close, but the journey down is steep and winding. **Mesa Mar** has a small beach and bars. Just beyond, along a pleasant coast road, is **El Pris**, a small bay with fish restaurants.

## West of Puerto de la Cruz

The motorway west of Puerto de la Cruz peters out at **Los Realejos**, which it divides between the older, upper part, Realejo Alto, and the lower, modern town, Realejo Bajo. This is the last chapter in the subjugation of the Guanches, where de Lugo pitched camp in 1498 and accepted the surrender of the remaining indigents and their lands. The much renovated church of Santiago Apóstol in the upper town still has the font where the converted Guanches were baptised.

Beyond Los Realejos is **San Juan de la Rambla**, an attractive, small white village by the sea. Inland, high above it, is La Guancha, a quiet artesanal village with fine views.

**Icod de los Vinos** ❾ is on the tourist map for its dragon tree, **El Drago Milenario**. Reaching 17m (56ft) with a 6m (20ft) circumference, it is the largest and most ancient on the island. It

## The dragon tree

The dragon tree (*Draecana draco*), which dates from the prehistoric Tertiary period, is unique to the Canary islands. It held a mystical quality for the Guanches, who saw it as a symbol of fertility and wisdom, using its bark on their shields when they went to war. Its resin, known as dragons' blood, turns red on contact with the air, and was used to embalm the Guanche dead. In Europe other uses were found for it, to dye hair golden, to stain marble red and to varnish violins.

stands by the main road on the west side of the town, helped in its old age by metal and concrete supports. Hard to date, it may not be quite the 1,000 years old that is claimed. Near the small park in which the tree stands is **Mariposario del Drago** (daily 10am–6pm in winter, until 7pm summer; www.mariposario.com), a tropical garden full of butterflies from around the world.

The dragon tree at Icod

The old town of Icod is one of the most attractive on the island. Its typical buildings are best around the Plaza de Constitución, shaded by palms, oleander and jacaranda, and in Plaza de la Pila, where the 19th-century Casa de los Cáceres is used as an exhibition centre. Icod has long been the centre of a wine-producing area, and you can buy its wares at the Casa del Vino in Plaza de Constitución. A wine festival takes place every year on the eve of St Andrew's Day (29 November), when locals ride on sleds down the steep streets of the town making as much noise as possible, in remembrance of the wine barrels once taken down to the port for export.

In a little square below the Plaza is the church of San Marcos, which contains a sacristy and small museum. Among its treasures is a filigree cross made of Mexican silver weighing 47kg (104lb). A much newer attraction in Icod is caving through volcanic lava tubes. The **Cueva del Viento** ❿ (www.cuevadelviento.net) has over 17km (11 miles) of lava tubes;

guided tours depart from the visitor centre (Tue–Sat 9am–4pm; tel: 922 815339, booking required).

Pinewoods behind the town stretch up towards El Teide. On the coast **Playa San Marcos** has an attractive small black beach with fishing boats and restaurants.

## EL TEIDE

The traditional path up to El Teide (it rhymes with 'lady') for early visitors to the island was from La Orotava. They would be taken by guides with mules up the track used by pumice miners and by the *neveros*, who brought ice down from the mountains to make ice cream.

Today there are four main roads up to the **Parque Nacional del Teide** ⓫ (www.parquesnacionalesdecanarias.es), so wherever you are on the island it is always accessible. Unless you are up for a five-hour climb, the last part of the journey has to be made by the Teleférico (cable car), 1.6km (1 mile) north of the Parador hotel and 8km (5 miles) south of the Visitor Centre. It does not operate during windy weather. You should arrive early in the morning to avoid queues. The highest mountain in Spain is 3,718m (12,198ft) above sea level and it is cold. Snow caps it for most of the year and temperatures can be well below freezing. Yet it is still surprising to learn how many of the 2.5 million people who visit the park each year turn up in beach wear.

Most people who alight from the cable car do not want to stroll far, and those who are pregnant or suffer from coronary or respiratory problems should not attempt to do so, as there is 50 percent less oxygen in the air than at sea level. It is possible to walk just beneath the crater.

### Shot on location

Since the 1966 movie *One Million Years BC*, starring Raquel Welch, El Teide's bleak lands have made an ideal backdrop for a number of science-fiction films.

El Teide, Spain's highest mountain

It is also possible to walk on its rim, but to prevent erosion from hikers' boots, the authorities have introduced a system whereby you have to have written permission to do this. Permits can be obtained free from the Parque Nacional del Teide on the fourth floor of Calle Emilio Calzadilla 5 in Santa Cruz (www.telefericoteide.com; tel: 922 010 440; Mon–Fri 9am–2pm). You will need to take your passport and show your free summit permit on the mountain top.

## Las Cañadas del Teide Crater

El Teide rises from a great hollow in the centre of the island, a caldera (a crater formed when the cone explodes) that is the remnants of an earlier, much larger volcano, of around 4,800m (16,000ft). This flat, pale expanse between the remnants of the former crater wall and the peak of El Teide forms the park. In fact there were two earlier volcanoes, creating two calderas, separated by the mauve and pink barrier of Los Roques de García. Together

People hike in the volcanic landscape of Teide National Park

they form an egg-shaped area 15km (9 miles) across. Lava and ashes have spilled from the volcanoes in a series of eruptions at different times, which explains why the rocks are so varied in texture and colour. Some cooled quickly into jagged formations, others cooled slowly into smoother, more liquid shapes.

El Teide lies to the north of the park and volcanic activity continues around the parasitic cones that sprouted around it. The most recent eruptions have formed a caldera on the summit of El Teide where fumaroles – escape hatches for steam – still blow. In 1798 an eruption created Las Narices del Teide (Teide's nostrils) on the south flank. The most recent eruption in the park occurred in 1909 from Montaña Chinyero, which is located in the west. El Teide is considered by experts to be still active.

A number of other volcanic peaks rise from the solidified lava in the park. Pico Viejo (3,134m/10,282ft) is to the southwest of El Teide and was formed a little earlier. The highest point on Las Cañadas del Teide's crater rim is Mt Guajara (2,717m/ 8,914ft) on the south side of the Parador hotel, and beyond it is the Paisaje Lunar, a haunting lunar landscape. To the north are the large caves of Cueva del Hielo or Cueva de los Cazadores. Around Guajara Pass, which once linked the Orotava road with Vilaflor, are former Guanche huts and many of the island's mummies have been found in caves nearby.

## The routes into the park

Once fertile lands scattered with small lakes, the calderas were the summer pastures for the Guanches' sheep and goats. They entered the region through *cañadas*, breaches in the rim of the calderas that give the park its name. These are most visible on the southern side where the Llano de Ucanca is the site of a former lake. The four modern roads into the park rise steeply and there are few other places on earth where the landscape changes so quickly, from lush valleys to the rocky, volcanic terrain of the higher elevations, passing through a cloud level between 1,000 and 1,500m (3,300–5,000ft).

### Climbing El Teide peak

The path to the summit starts approximately 2km (1 mile) east of the Teleférico (cable car) base, where there is parking space for about a dozen cars and a map of the route. It is a straight walk up, with no scrambling or climbing, and it takes about five hours, during which you will climb around 1,400m (4,600ft). You can return via the Teleférico. A fleece and waterproof jacket are recommended, and in winter you should also wear snow glasses. Camping is not allowed in the park, but there is a refuge, the Refugio de Altavista, at 3,250m (10,650ft). Just beyond the refuge is a 19th-century ice cave, where early visitors cooled themselves after the horse ride up from La Orotava.

As the path reaches the top of the Teleférico, you will need to present your permit (see page 55) and passport to a ranger before continuing along the Telesforo Bravo path to the rim of the crater, through fumaroles emitting sulphurous clouds. The view is absolutely spectacular, and on a clear day you should be able to see all of the Canary Islands.

## From the north

The road that leads from La Orotava twists and climbs steeply through the moist Orotava Valley, past thatched barns and patches of agricultural land towards the village of **Aguamansa**. Here, there are forest trails through the pines, and aviaries in which sick or wounded birds are taken care of. The village is situated in the cloud level, so if you plan to go for a walk, be prepared for some precipitation. Nearby is **Los Organos**, rock formations that look like organ pipes. Beyond Aguamansa look for another geological curiosity on the left-hand side of the road, the **Marguerita de Piedra**, a lump of basalt rock that seems to have exploded, forming daisy-like petals. Finally, at 2,020m (6,630ft), the road is joined by the road from La Laguna and it enters the park at the Portillo Pass.

The cable car

## From the east

The road from La Laguna is also the best route from Santa Cruz, so it can be busy at weekends. Built in the 1940s by the military, this road is the straightest, least steep of the four, running along the ridge of the Cum bre Dorsal and providing spectacular views over both coasts. It passes through **La Esperanza**, a place known for its roadside meat restaurants. From here the **Bosque la Esperanza**, a forest of pines and picnic spots, spreads beside the road for a dozen kilometres. On the left, before the first view-point at **Mirador de las Flores**, is **Las Raíces**, the spot where Franco and a hundred co-conspirators met at an outdoor lunch in June 1939 to seal their agreements shortly before their attack on the mainland. A monument marks the spot.

At 2,400m (7,900ft) the road reaches two sky-watching insti-tutions, the **Observatorio Atmosférico de Izaña** (http://izana.aemet.es) and the **Observatorio Astronómico del Teide** (guided tours by appointment only, tel: 922 329 110, book at www.volcanolife.com). Increasing light pollution on the island has affected their usefulness.

## The starting point

As the peak comes dramatically into view, the road from La Laguna meets the one from La Orotava at **El Portillo** just before the **Visitor Centre** (daily 9am–4pm). Moroccan cedars have been introduced here as part of an attempt to replant deforested areas. Measures to conserve the nature of the park have meant that many paths are closed to vehicles and hikers. Essential maps and guides should be on sale here, but don't count on them being in stock: if you are walking, it is best to try to find decent maps before reaching the park. Videos and displays give a good grounding in the history of the park and an idea of what to expect. Some tours and guides are advertised or may be avail-able. You can also check out the flora here: Teide daisies flower in the winter snow, pink broom blossoms in May, and the Teide violet a little later. The rock's colour depends on the time of day and the light: the lava is in extraordinary hues of yellows, reds and browns, and there's the shiny black obsidian with which the Guanche made blades for their tools and weapons.

## Cable car and Parador hotel

From the Visitor Centre it is about 12km (7 miles) to the **Teleférico** or cable car. It runs up the mountain from 9am

View from the top of El Teide

to 4pm (with the last chance to come down again at 4.50pm), takes eight minutes, and stops 170m (560ft) short of the summit. Refreshments are available at the bottom only. Paths from the top lead to two miradors at the foot of the final ascent, for which you need a permit (see page 55). From the viewpoints you can see the jagged rocky and rope-like formations from the mountain's latest lava flows.

The **Parador Las Cañadas del Teide** (see page 135) is the only hotel in the park and it makes an excellent base for an early start to walk to the summit. The night sky is sparkling, and groups of visitors come to the Parador for dinner and astronomy talks. Nearby are **Los Roques de García** ⑫, extraordinary gnarled formations that are all that is left of the dividing wall between the two former volcanoes that make up the caldera. They are among the most photographed phenomenon in the park. Stones near these rocks are deep green from copper oxide, and are known as **Los Azulejos**, the glazed tiles.

## From the southwest

From Playa de las Américas, Los Cristianos and the other resorts of the southwest, the 90-minute drive up to the park starts either at Arona or at Granadilla de Abona, and climbs steeply to where the roads converge at **Vilaflor ⑬**. Situated at an altitude of 1,400m (4,600ft), this village claims to be the highest in Spain, and its population of 1,800 makes it the island's smallest municipality. It stands among volcanic cones in the middle of pine woods, of which the Pino Gordo, the fat pine, is the finest example, 65m (215ft) tall and 10m (30ft) in circumference. Vilaflor is a good base for exploring the mountains and is the nearest village to the park, where there are no shops or commercial outlets. Its 16th-century church was founded by a Catalan colonialist, Pedro Soler, who first put this land to work for the Spanish. Vilaflor is a popular stopping point, so if you wish to stay here, try to book a hotel in advance.

It is noticeably cooler here than on the coast and it snows in winter. Generally, however, when the weather is poor on the coast, it is sunny up here above the clouds. The bare earth on the tidy, geometrical terraces is covered with lava pebbles called *picón*, which help to hold in the moisture. There is no shortage of water, and underground springs provide the island with bottled water. There is also enough moisture for a healthy agricultural industry of tomatoes, potatoes and grapes. These must be among the highest vineyards in the world and their white wines are increasingly talked about.

Los Roques de García

Echium wildpretii (red bugloss)
growing on El Teide

Just outside Vilaflor is the **Ermita San Roque** with a mirador and the Restaurant El Mirador, which makes a good stopping place. This is followed by two more miradors beside the road, **Mirador de las Pinos** and, just beyond a large bottling plant, **Mirador las Lajas**. Both make pleasant picnic stops.

## From the west

The road from the west coast rises from the white village of **Chio** at 680m (2,240ft), from where there is a panoramic view back over the coast around the high cliffs of Los Gigantes. Less twisting than the road through Vilaflor, it climbs through the inhospitable, jagged clinker and dark grey lava to reach the road from Vilaflor at **Boca de Tauce**. Here a breach in the caldera rim lets the road through into the lunar landscape of the park.

## THE NORTHWEST

The northwest of the island is one of its richest and most diverse areas. Deeply rural, it has many hidden corners as well as popular spots, none of which are ever very crowded. Much of the area is covered by **El Teno Rural Park ⓮**, a conservation area of more than 80sq km (30sq miles) based on the Teno massif, one of the geologically oldest parts of the island. There is a range of vegetation between the hills and valleys, and wild flowers are in abundance. Bird life is also plentiful, both in the hills and around the northern coastal plain, and sea birds can be seen from Punto El Teno. **Isla Baja** is the name given to the region that covers the districts of Buenavista, Garachico, Los Silos and El Tanque. Its capital is Garachico, which makes a good base.

A number of traditional houses and *fincas* (country estates) throughout the region have been converted into places to stay.

## Garachico

An hour before dawn on 5 May 1709, the sky above **Garachico** ⓯ was lit up by the eruption of El Volcán Negro, 8km (5 miles) inland. It was not long before two streams of lava were scorching their way through forests and vineyards towards the coast. Alarmed, the people of Garachico, Tenerife's main port, watched it coming. Genoese merchants abandoned their mansions and monks and nuns left their religious houses, fleeing the path of the boiling lava. In the harbour, ships trading in sugar and wine could only put to sea and watch as the river of molten earth barged and burned its way through the town's buildings and filled up the harbour, turning the sea into a boiling cauldron. Garachico's days of glory were over, and it would never be the same again.

Castillo de San Miguel, Garachico

If you go up to the **Mirador de Garachico** you can look down on the white buildings that cover the curve of lava jutting out into the sea and make out the paths of the two devastating rivers of molten rock.

Garachico today is a handsome town of over 5,000 that is so unhurried that it needs no traffic lights. Its seafront is given over to leisure, with a municipal pool, a football pitch and a modern marina. Once or twice a year the sea comes in and batters the pitch, though most days the blue water looks benign, especially where it laps the black swimming rocks around the **Castillo de San Miguel** (www.castillosanmiguel.com). With its bar and restaurant, this is a good place to look out across the sea as the sun sets. The castle, dating from 1570, has a collection of shells from around the world, and provides a viewing point from its battlements.

Santa Ana in Garachico

Just inland from the castle is the pretty **Plaza de Juan Gonzales de la Torre**, at the back of which the former land gate to the harbour has been excavated. There is a huge 17th-century wine press here, too, a reminder of the time when locally produced Malvasia wine made Garachico – and Tenerife – rich. Nearby is a monument to Cristóbal de Ponte, the Genoan banker who founded the town. A few steps from the square is the parish church of

**Santa Ana**. Rebuilt after the eruption, it contains a magnificent crucifix by Martin de Andujar, a Sevillian craftsman, and a figure of Christ made by Tarasco Indians in Mexico. Beside the church, the small curved Calle Esteban de Ponte follows the seafront. The de Ponte family house is located here, and other impressive 17th *century* buildings include the restaurant Pensión El Jardín, which is opposite the tourist information office.

Old architecture in Garachico

The main square, Plaza de la Libertad, which remains much as it must have looked before the eruption, is shaded and has a small café. A statue of the Venezuelan revolutionary leader, Simón Bolívar, has been added because his mother, María Concepción Palacio y Blanco, was born in the town. It was the first statue of the great liberator to be erected in Spain. On the southern side of the square is the palace of the counts of Gomera. Dominating the eastern side is the church of **Nuestra Señora de los Angeles** and the 18th-century former **Convento de San Francisco**. The latter has two fine courtyards and is home to the **Casa de la Cultura**, where exhibitions are held, and a small natural history museum. On the northern side are the ochre walls of La Quinta Roja (see page 139), a beautiful hotel with a bar and restaurant. It is also a centre of activities in the region, with information on walks and tours. Drop in to find out what is going on – and look out for the turtles in the garden.

Another smart hotel is the San Roque (see page 138), in the Casa Noriega just to the west of the square, and its contemporary sculptures show the town's fondness for the arts as well as its heritage.

## West of Garachico

The road heading west out of Garachico goes past the **Playa del Muelle** and up to a headland where the **Monumento a los Emigrantes Canarios** shows a figure with a suitcase and a hole in his heart setting off for a better life in America. There has been large scale emigration from this corner of the island, especially to Venezuela, and many towns and villages celebrate the day of Nuestra Señora de Buen Viaje, Our Lady of the Good Journey, on 31 August.

Monument to the Emigrants

The nearest good beach to Garachico is a little further on, the **Playa La Caleta de Interián**.

As the road heads west, the countryside starts to flatten, smoothing a path first through sleepy **Los Silos** and arriving at **Buenavista del Norte**. Built around a central square with a small pavilion, its low, white houses have a languid, southern feel. The church of Nuestra Señora de los Remedios was refurbished after a serious fire in 1966.

The road leading from Buenavista continues all the way to **Faro del Teno** ⓰, the lighthouse at the island's northwestern tip, which attracts birdwatchers on the lookout for ospreys, Barbary falcons and Cory's shearwaters. Road signs warn motorists of the dangers of landslides, which tend to occur mainly in windy and wet weather. La Gomera and La Palma are in view as you reach the headland, and at the lighthouse at **Punto del Teno** you can see down the entire west coast.

From Buenavista the road heads inland, past vines and signs for cheese for sale, and up through a changing mass of vegetation, with poppies lining the road. Among geological curiosities is the **Montañeta del Palmer**, which has been sliced like a cake for the extraction of *picón*, a gravel made of lava which is spread on agricultural land to retain moisture in the soil.

At the **Mirador del Baracán** there is a view down over both coasts. Bees hum as they potter about the aromatic plants, swifts dart overhead and there are walking paths off into Teno Park.

## Masca

The jewel of Tenerife's northwest is **Masca ⑰**, a cluster of buildings tipped over the side of the hill in a stunning setting above the sea. Approached over the hills from Buenavista or along the dramatic ribbon of road that flutters down from Santiago del Teide, Masca is not much more than a hamlet.

It has approximately 100 inhabitants and it was off the tourist map until the road to it was eventually constructed in 1972.

Near the roadside, where cars squeeze into the few parking spaces, there are a couple of restaurants with terraces where you can eat cactus ice cream with goat's yoghurt and honey, or suck cactus and papaya juice

The hamlet of Masca

through a straw. Among the clutch of attractive buildings just below is a small museum of local finds.

The forest fires of July 2007, which burnt more than 15,000 hectares (37,000 acres) of land, engulfed the town and destroyed half the buildings. Fortunately no lives were lost as the village was evacuated in time. Houses have been restored and the valley is greening up. Located in a traditional house, a small **Museo Etnográfico** (Mon–Sat 11am–5pm) offers a glimpse into the life of the town's former inhabitants. One of the main draws is the six-hour round hike into the narrow **Barranco de Masca** and down to the beach. After being damaged in the fire, the wooden bridge was replaced by a new metal one and the path has been reopened to hikers. If you prefer to skip the trek back uphill, there are tour boats to Los Gigantes (last boat 4.30pm).

## El Tanque

The road above the coast at Garachico leads to **El Tanque**, a district of five hamlets scattered among pastureland in patchworks of fields between sweeping mountains. The main village of El Tanque overlooks the sea and centres on a corn exchange, the Casa de la Alhóndiga, that was once the town's meeting place. Mirador Lomo Molino is yet another great viewpoint on this route.

Church in Santiago del Teide

Continuing along this road, it is something of a surprise to see blue-robed 'bedouins' in camel trains. The **Camello Center** (Carretera General TF-82 km 10,2; www.camellocenter.es; tel:

922 136191; daily 9.30am–5pm) offers donkeys as well as camels for hire on half-hour excursions.

The road now climbs to reach the **Erjos** mountain pass (1,117m/3,664ft), where paths lead down to old farmhouses in the valleys. This pass divides north from south, and from here the full southern heat brings only cacti and *malpaís* to the dry scrubland. It meets the road up from Masca at **Santiago del Teide**, a sunny white town in a broad valley. To the east is **Montaña del Chinyero**, the last volcano to erupt on the island, in 1909.

Los Gigantes Harbour

The village of **Arguayo**, situated just beyond, is famous for its ceramics, and includes the **Centro Alfarero y Museo Etnográfico Cha Domitila** (Tue–Sat 10am–1pm and 4–7pm, Sun 10am–2pm), a museum and workshop showcasing traditional earthenware.

## Los Gigantes to San Juan

Boats that sail to Masca bay are just part of the flotilla of pleasure craft berthed in **Los Gigantes** ⓲. This port, at the bottom of a steep hill, is the island's premier diving centre (see page 87) and the possibilities for water activities are endless. The port looks directly out at the *acantilado*, the cliff that rises sheer in front of it – this is the dramatic 800m (2,625ft) wall of the Teno massif, where the boat-less Guanche thought that

## Row the Atlantic

One of the world's toughest sporting events is the Atlantic Rowing Challenge. 5,000 km (3,000 miles) from Los Gigantes to Barbados. Boats 7.3m (24ft) long are rowed by two oarsmen. Chay Blythe started the race in 1997, 30 years after his three-month trans-Atlantic crossing with John Ridgeway.

the world came to an abrupt end. The cliff also drops fairly rapidly beneath the sea, making deep diving possible.

Los Gigantes' tiny beach has been sealed off since a landslide in 2009, but there is a good swimming pool, Piscina la Laguillo, just up from the port and a much larger beach, **Playa de Arena**, at its sister resort, **Puerto Santiago**, which is within easy striking distance. You might also take a dip at Oasis pool, which boasts a short slide, splendid views of the cliffs and a restaurant. The next resort of **Alcalá**, also based on a fishing port, has natural pools to swim in. **San Juan**, about 8km (5 miles) south of Los Gigantes, manages to retain its character as a working fishing port, despite the new development. Around the bay, a sand beach has been created. On Wednesday and Sunday mornings a food and craft market attracts visitors from around the region. There are also a couple of snorkelling and scuba diving schools offering the chance to see rays, cuttlefish and octopus.

Inland from San Juan is **Guía de Isora**, a rural community where potatoes and tomatoes grow. Its church has two Madonnas by José Luján Pérez.

## THE SOUTH

Served by Reina Sofia airport, the south of the island is where it is hot, so this is where holidaymakers go, mainly to the resorts in the *municipios* of Adeje and Arona, in the merged touristopolis of Playa de las Américas and Los Cristianos. Hotels, apartments and villas continue to spread along the coast, bringing greenery to the *malpaís*, the badlands. Near the airport is the longest beach on the island, El Médano. All along the shore back towards Santa Cruz are rocky bays and small fishing ports such as Los Abrigos and Abona. An upper road, from Granadilla de Abona to Güímar, where Thor Heyerdahl discovered mystic 'pyramids', passes through some small villages with views all down the coast. Some 15km (10 miles) before Santa Cruz the road drops to the coast around Candelaria, the most important pilgrimage town in the Canary Islands.

## The big resorts

You have to know where you are going when you arrive in **Playa de las Américas** ⑲. Built out of nothing in the 1970s, it has no natural centre, the roads are often not signposted and directions are generally given by the names of hotels. Most

Sunlounging in the south

Palm trees in Playa de las Américas

of the seafront belongs to the four- and five-star hotels and often the closest you will get to the beach in a vehicle is their car parks.

On the seafront you can see the spectacular hotel fantasies that make up various people's ideas of heaven, from Canarian villages to Mexican *haciendas*, courtesans' boudoirs and the glories of ancient Rome. Most ambitious is **Mare Nostrum** (www.expohotels.com; see page 141), a 'resort' of five-star hotels that look like something out of a Cecile B. de Mille epic. It includes the Mediterranean Palace, the Cleopatra Palace and Sir Anthony hotels – all three offering pools, bars and restaurants. The large **Playa de las Vistas** lies between here and Los Cristianos but the main beaches of **Playas de Troya** and **Playa del Bobo** are to the north of the **Barranco del Rey**. There is a tourist information point at this gully, which is near the rowdy **Veronicas** strip, a hub of more than 100 nightclubs. Technically the *barranco* marks the municipal boundary between Arona and Adeje. The coast north of here is the rapidly developing **Costa Adeje**, which drifts seamlessly into the giant hotels of San Eugenio, Torviscas, Fañabe, Playa del Duque, Playa Paraiso and Calle Salvaje. The small harbour of **Puerto Colón** in San Eugenio is the centre for water activities, dolphin and whale-watching boats, and diving (see page 88). Inland

from the port is a large **Aqualand** water park (www.aqualand.
es), just one of myriad activities.

There are no limits to entertainment possibilities in and
around Playa de las Américas (see page 93). On Thursdays
and Saturdays follow the crowds to the market held near Plaza
del Duque at the north of the resort. The plaza itself is home
to a shopping centre, with upmarket boutiques as well as
chain stores such as Mango.

**La Caleta** just to the north of Playa del Duque is quickly
developing, but the waterfront is still an enticing spot for its
seafood restaurants.

## Los Cristianos

The starting point of these resorts was the port of **Los Cristianos**
❷⓪, which lies on the south side of Playa de las Américas. They
are separated by the volcanic cone of Montaña Chayofita, but it
is otherwise hard to see the join, and you can walk from one to
the other along a 7km (4-mile), palm-lined promenade, dotted
with pizzerias and souvenir shops. The port is still active, its ferries serving the neighbouring islands of El Hierro, La Palma and

### Siam Park

Siam Park (daily May–Oct 10am-6pm, till 5pm in winterwww.siampark.
net), opened on the Costa Adeje in 2008. This Thai-themed park boasts
state-of-the-art water rides set within exotic gardens and a massive
white sand beach. Adrenalin junkies are likely to head for the Tower of
Power with its almost vertical 28m (92ft) drop, climaxing in a tube of
swimming alligators and tropical fish. Surfers can enjoy the wave palace
with 3m (10ft) -high manmade waves. For those looking for something
more relaxing there are sunbeds on the beach. A combination ticket
with Loro Parque is available, and there is free bus transport from Los
Cristianos, Playa de la Américas and Costa Adeje.

La Gomera. The south-facing **Playa los Cristianos** and **Playa de las Vistas** are sheltered and the sea is shallow and safe. Mar de Ons, a kiosk on Playa de Vistas, offers numerous sea excursions, including deep-sea fishing and a pirate boat cruise (www.mardeons-tenerife.com). Puerto Colón is the main departure point for whale- and dolphin-watching trips (see page 88).

Los Cristianos has an authentic atmosphere, especially around its main pedestrian street, Avenida de Suecia, where there are inexpensive *pensións*, and above the Paseo Marítimo, where a row of restaurants and bars offer sea views. Events and exhibitions are staged in the **Centro Cultural** where the tourist office is situated. At the far end of the beach an open area is the site of a lively Sunday market. Alternatively, take TF-655 and then TF-28 to Chayofa with its nearby Jungle Park (daily 10am–4.30pm; www.aguilasjunglepark.com), which is home to more than 300 animals including penguins, sea lions, wild cats and birds. There are twice daily shows featuring birds of prey as well as sea lions.

## La Gomera

Christopher Columbus's last port of call before he headed into the unknown in 1492 was the island of La Gomera, now just 30 minutes away from Los Cristianos on Fred Olsen's Australian-built *Benchijigua*. When you step ashore at San Sebastián you will find yourself in quite a different world. This quiet, underpopulated island is just 24km (15 miles) across, but you need to get away from the port to find its rural secrets. At its centre is the Parque Nacional de Garajonay, a Unesco World Heritage Site, which you pass through to get to the lovely Valle de Gran Rey. For the sunniest beach, take a bus to Playa de Santiago. One of the world's toughest sporting events, the Talisker Whisky Atlantic Challenge takes off from San Sebastián every December, when oarsmen teams in 7.3m (24ft) boats attempt to row 5,000 km (3,000 miles) across the Atlantic to Antigua.

## The municipal towns

Inland are the municipality's main towns, Adeje and Arona. **Adeje**, the former seat of the Guanche government, has never minded much how it made money. At the top of the town are the remains of the **Casa Fuerte**, the stronghold of Pedro, Count of Gomera and one of the Genoese de Ponte family, who ruled the roost along this coast. He fell in with another rogue, the Elizabethan pirate John Hawkins, and together they conducted illegal trade with South America, as well as legitimately dealing in African slaves. Hawkins, who was later knighted for his role in defeating the Spanish Armada, was the first Englishman to become involved in the slave trade, in 1562. The town has a pleasant, if steep Rambla, lined with bars and cafés, that leads to the Iglesia Santa Ursula, with a Gobelins tapestry among its contents and an 18th-century chapel that was once part of a Franciscan convent.

San Sebastian de la Gomera's promenade

Turn left at the top of the Rambla for the Casa Fuerte, and then up to Otelo, the restaurant at the entry point to the **Barranco del Infierno** (tel: 922 78 28 85; daily 8.30am– 2.30pm; www.barrancodelinfierno.es; visitors are advised to reserve in advance as numbers to the gorge are limited to 200), one of the most dramatic ravines on the island and the main reason that so many visitors come to the town. Stout shoes and at least 1 litre of water per person are needed for the round-trip walk up to the waterfall at the head of the *barranco*, which takes around three hours. There is a surprising amount of plant life along the way. If nothing else, this walk can give those staying at the main resorts a flavour of the island's true nature.

## Along the south coast

New developments continue around the southern tip of the island, at **Palm Mar** and the **Costa del Silencio**, which are entirely purpose-built communities. Between the two is **Las Galletas**, a little fishing port swamped by hotels and apartments, but where fish is still sold on the quayside every morning, bringing many *tinerfeños* in search of a good catch. The seafront is a pleasant stroll, with delicious Italian ice creams at Yo-Yo. At the Colibri restaurant you can eat fresh fish, *azul* or *blanca* (oily or white), by the kilo.

Perhaps the best place for fish restaurants is **Los Abrigos**, the next port along, where restaurants line the lane leading down to the port and hospitable women invite you in to dine.

The longest beach in Tenerife stretches several kilometres around the **Montaña Roja**, a volcanic lump that punctuates the bleak acres of arid coast by the airport. Cars line the road but there are few amenities on the khaki-coloured sand, which stretches from the naturist beach of **La Tejita** to the small port of **El Médano** ㉑. Many visitors come here in search of good waves, for this is the haunt of serious windsurfers, and major championships have been held with the aid

Surfers off El Médano

Montaña Roja near El Médano, visible from Reina Sofia airport

of the *alisios*, the steady northeast trade winds. The building that breaks the beachscape is the Playa Sur Tenerife (www. hotelplayasurtenerife.com; see page 139) that has been catering to windsurfers for decades. El Médano, at the end of the beach, has accommodation and restaurants.

Further along is **Poris de Abona**, a small community with seafood restaurants and a little beach but increasing development.

## Granadilla de Abona to Güímar

Just outside El Médano on the road up to Granadilla de Abona is the **Cueva del Hermano Pedro**, the cave where the shepherd boy Peter de Betancurt prayed as a child. Of Norman descent, Brother Peter was born on 19 March 1626, at Vilaflor. At 23 he left for the Americas where he became a missionary in Guatemala and did charitable work among the poor, for which he was canonised in 2002. The cave is now a pilgrim site.

Church in Granadilla de Abona

The old town of **Granadilla de Abona** ㉒ can seem deserted after the clamour of the coast. Clock chimes emanate from the central church, dedicated to St Anthony of Padua. A number of the houses in the old town have been restored, especially in Calle Arquitecto Morrero, just down from the church, where one has become a *casa rural*. Next door is the small **Museo de la Historia de Granadilla de Abona** (Mon–Fri 8am–3pm; free), a museum of local history.

The upper road continues through sleepy old villages surrounded by terraced fields, many of them abandoned. At **Arico el Nuevo** there is also a sense of desertion, of pretty old buildings done up and awaiting some purpose.

The road dives in and out of a succession of deep gullies, the *barrancos*. Pigeons and doves of every colour appreciate the rocks for nesting, while the larger caves have been put to good use as storage space. At the **Mirador de Don Martín** there is a view over the Valle de Güímar where pineapple, avocado, banana, chirimoya, guava, cereal and vines are cultivated.

## Ancient temples

Some of the dry stone terraces here, known as *molleros* or *majones*, look like the bases of pyramids and it is no surprise to find the **Parque Etnográfico Pirámides de Güímar** ㉓ (www.piramidesdeguimar.es; daily 9.30am–6pm) above the town of Güímar. This park is the work of an extraordinary man, Thor Heyerdahl, who lived in Tenerife from 1994 until his death in 2002. In that time he discovered what he believed to be the Guanches' cult of building flat-topped, step-sided pyramids for sun worship. Ship-owner and fellow Norwegian, Fred Olsen, bought land for the park and helped to develop it into a research centre.

Through Heyerdahl's expeditions on the balsa raft *Kon-Tiki* and the reed raft *Ra*, he made connections between the civilisations of Egypt and Mexico. Several acres of buildings have been uncovered. Replicas of his rafts are on show, and the links between the indigenous peoples of North Africa, the Americas and the Pacific are speculated upon in a museum.

**Güímar** is a working town of 15,000, known for its wines and traditional, male-dominated *tascas* (see page 103). It has two good churches, both with coffered *mudéjar* ceilings. The parish church at the top of the town has an exceptionally elaborate silver altarpiece, and the curiously arranged church

Parque Etnográfico Pirámides de Güímar

of San Domingo, in the former monastery of the same name, is by the town hall in a shady square.

The tourist office is in the Casa de Artesana on the main shopping street, where you can find information on walks in the Malpaís de Güímar. This semi-desert wasteland surrounds the Montaña Grande below the town and spreads down to **Puertito de Güímar** on the coast. Here there is a pebble beach, and outside the town, in the direction of the Club Náutico (www.nauticoguimar.com), you'll find a sandy shore.

## Candelaria

The name Candelaria, 'giver of light', means only one thing in the Canary Islands: a venerated Madonna, who is the islands' patron saint. The town of **Candelaria** ㉔, on the coast, is dominated by the 1950s basilica (Tue–Sun 7.30am–7.30pm, Mon 3–7.30pm; free) that contains her image, and thousands of pilgrims gather in the square outside every August on the Feast of the Assumption, when the conversion of the Guanches to Christianity is re-enacted.

Lining the sea side of the square are statues by José

Guanche chiefs, Candelaria

Abad of the seven Guanche *menceys*, or chiefs, who were in power at the time of de Lugo's conquest. Six of them didn't have too much to be thankful for when Christianity arrived. One, however, the *mencey* of Güímar, was already half way to becoming a Christian without realising it. Inside the church the story of the discovery of the

Madonna and her healing powers is told in delightful but murky paintings. They show the wooden Madonna holding Jesus in one hand and a candle in the other, arriving on the shore in 1392. Two shepherds discovered her, and one of them cut his hand on his knife while trying to ascertain if the statue was alive. The wound stopped bleeding the moment he touched her. When news got out, the *mencey* of Güímar, who was the shepherd's leader, had a shrine built for the Madonna, and when the Spanish conquerors arrived, they convinced him that his conversion was underway. De Lugo was thus able to

Interior of the Basilica of Nuestra Senora de la Candelaria, located in Candelaria

persuade him to join the Spaniards in their subjugation of the island's pagan Guanche tribes.

As well as an interesting ceramics workshop and museum (Centro Alfarero de Candelaria, Calle Isla de la Gomera 7, Tue–Fri 9.30am–2pm, Wed and Fri 5–8pm, Sat 10am–4pm), try to catch the large, bustling craft market in the main square (every other Fri 11am–9pm). An agricultural market is held every Wednesday (4–9pm), while flea market on Sunday (8am–9pm).

The tourist office, in Plaza CIT, has information on the town as well as walks into the surrounding countryside.

# WHAT TO DO

Tenerife's highlights and attractions lie in its natural resources. With a pleasant climate and a diverse landscape of dramatic coasts and exotic interior, the island is ideal for all kinds of outdoor activities. Many visitors come here to walk in the hills and enjoy the abundant flora and search out unique fauna. Much of the island is given over to parks and nature reserves. The sea, dropping steeply to the depths of the Atlantic, is a favourite for both experienced and novice divers, and there are whales and dolphins to watch if you don't want to get wet.

## OUTDOOR ACTIVITIES

### Walking and hiking

The island is crossed by a large number of tracks and footpaths including a growing number of designated walking routes. Tourist offices provide free leaflets on walks in the Orotava Valley, the Anaga Hills and Teno Rural Park. More ambitious walkers, who have no coronary or respiratory concerns, will want to conquer the lavascapes of the *cañadas* around El Teide, and information can be found at the information centre for the Parque Nacional de las Cañadas del Teide (see page 54). Walking maps, guides and books, often in English, can be found in bookshops *(librerías)*. Cruz del Carmen Mirador (daily 9.30am–4pm) has information on walking in the Anaga Hills, where the Albergue Montes de Anaga (www.albergues-tenerife.net; see page 134) makes a good base. Other hotels that make good bases for walking are La Quinta Roja in Garachico (see page 139) for the northwest and the VillAlba

Windsurfer picking up the trade winds at El Médano

Cycling by El Teide

Spa Hotel (http://hotelesreveron.com) in Vilaflor for the southwest (see page 141).

Patea Tus Montes (www.pateatusmontes.com; tel: 922 33 59 03) offer hikes around the island guided by locals, as well as climbing and mountain biking.

You can also plan walks before you go by checking out www.webtenerife.com or www.todotenerife.com.

## Bikes and karting

Mountain bikes can be hired in main tourist centres. Try Rafting Bike (www.raftingbike.com; tel: 699 94 46 22) if you don't fancy all that pedalling. Trips are downhill all the way, starting at 2,250 metres (7,400ft) and travelling 35km (22 miles) down to the sea. Club Activo Cycling (www.clubactivocycling.com) offers bike rental (also electric ones) as well as tours for different levels ranging from one to seven days.

Motorbikes can also be hired. Bikes range from 50cc scooters (€20 a day) to 650cc models at 85 a day. Check Motorcycle Hire Tenerife (http://motorcyclehire-tenerife.com) or Rentalmotorbike (www.rentalmotorbike.com)

Quad bikes can be ridden in Quad Park in Arona, opposite Aqualand, or at Quad Safari (www.www.quad-tenerife.com).

Jeep tours are available from Tamarán Alquiler Jeep Safari in Playa de las Américas (www.tamaran.com; tel: 922 79 47 57).

## Flora spotting

The flora, which brightens the island throughout the year, is one of the reasons for visiting Tenerife. May and June, when the roadsides are overwhelmed with flowers, are the best months to come, but there is something to see all year round. Flora endemic to the island can be found in many different habitats. Cañada del Teide supports alpine plants such as the Teide echium ('The Pride of Tenerife'), while desert-like species are found around El Médano in the *malpaís* lands of the south. Some of these are very rare, and no fewer than 19 plants have been identified as now being under threat.

When the islands were used as a staging post between the New World and Spain, many South American species were introduced. Some can be seen at the Jardín Botánico in Puerto de la Cruz. The hotel Jardín Tropical in Playa de las Américas also has a substantial collection.

The Museo de la Naturaleza y el Hombre (www.museosde tenerife.org) in Santa Cruz gives an account of the island's flora, and its shop has several books and charts on the subject.

## Birdwatching

The island is not abundant with birds, but there are some unusual ones that can be seen, particularly those unique to the island (see page 12). The best places to view seabirds are around the lighthouses on the three extreme points of the island (Faro de Teno, Faro de la Rasca and Faro de Anaga).

Look out for notices about organised local walks. Recommended books include: *A*

Mountain flora on El Teide

*Birdwatcher's Guide to the Canary Islands* by Tony Clarke and David Collins, *Finding Birds in the Canary Islands* by Dave Gosney and *Where to Watch Birds in Tenerife* by Eduardo García del Rey.

## Horse and camel riding

Stables offering hacks through the countryside include La Caldera del Rey (www.tenerifehorses.com; tel: 648 650 441) at Costa Adeje, and El Rancho Grande (www.amarillagolf.es) at the Amarilla Golf and Country Club . Both cater for children and adults. You might also try Centro Hípico del Sur (www.centrohipicodelsur.com). Donkeys as well as camels can be hired at the Camello Center (www.camellocenter.es) in El Tanque (with other branches in Puerto de la Cruz and Adeje), in the northwest.

## Golf

Tenerife has nine golf courses and several hotels with golf packages. One of Spain's oldest courses the Real Club de Golf de Tenerife (www.rcgt.es), is the island's longest-established, opened in 1932. Found near Los Rodeos airport and blessed with good views, it looks rather like an English park. The other course in the north is the Buenavista (www.buenavistagolf.es), designed by Seve Ballesteros. Courses in the south include Golf Las Américas (www.golf-tenerife.com), Golf Costa Adeje (www.golfcostaadeje.com), Golf del Sur (www.golfdelsur.net) and the Amarilla Golf and Country Club (www.amarillagolf.es); the latter two are both in San Miguel de Abona.

### Hang-gliding

There are more than 40 high spots for hang-gliders to jump from. Courses and flights (also double-seater) are available at Tenerfly (Calle Reykjavik, Adeje, tel: 637 559 222; www.tenerfly.com). The Canary Island Air Sports Federation (FECDA; www.fecda.org) offers detailed information on paragliding routes in Tenerife.

# WATER ACTIVITIES

Just about every waterborne activity ever thought of is available on the west and south coasts of the island. Some, like whale-watching and scuba diving, allow you to experience the area's unique wildlife, whilst others, such as windsurfing, take advantage of the superb natural conditions.

Kitesurfing is becoming popular

## Diving

The waters around the island swiftly drop to dramatic depths, with caves, caverns and a diversity of ocean life that have made Tenerife dive sites some of the most popular in the world. Sea temperatures are conducive year-round, from an average 20°C (68°F) in winter to 24°C (75°F) in summer. Tuna, barracuda, sting rays, eagle rays and morays are among the big fish; rainbow wrasse and trigger fish are among the small delights. Sponges, anemones, and red and yellow gorgonias also lie in wait. Though the waters plunge to 2,000m (6,500ft), there is a legal depth of 40m (130ft) imposed on dives, many of which are multi-level. Operators offer equipment and courses from beginner to divemaster, as well as video and film-making possibilities. Note that Spanish law precludes under-16s from scuba diving. Most diving centres operate on the west coast, with companies concentrated in Los Gigantes (Los

Gigantes Dive Center; www.divingtenerife.co.uk; tel: 922 86 0431), Playa San Juan, Los Cristianos and around the corner in Las Galletas (Buceo Tenerife Diving Center; www.buceo tenerife.com; tel: 922 73 1015).

## Whale- and dolphin-watching

The clear, warm waters between Tenerife and La Gomera are home to pilot whales and bottlenose dolphins which can be seen all year round. Half-day trips in catamarans are organized by a number of companies including Freebird (www. freebirdone.com) and Lady Shelley (www.ladyshelley.com).

Two glass-bottom catamarans, the *Tropical Delfin* and *Royal Delfin* (www.tenerifedolphin.com; tel: 922 750 085), operate out of Puerto Colón. The owners of the wooden sailing boat *Katrin* (www.dolphinwhalewatch.com), based in Los Gigantes, conduct ethical dolphin-watching tours, mooring off Masca Bay, where you can snorkel from the boat (tel: 922 860 332). You can also book a trip through Whales and Dolphins Tenerife (http://whalesanddolphinsoftenerife.org).

## Big-game fishing

Shark, blue marlin, tuna and barracuda are the big game to be fished off the west coast. Boats can be hired in Los Gigantes, Playa San Juan or Los Cristianos.

### Sea safety

Swimming in the sea is relatively safe around the island on the designated beaches, but currents and waves can develop, creating powerful undertows. Look out for a red flag flown, indicating that conditions are unsafe for swimming.

## Windsurfing

Windsurfers head for El Médano, where the bay between the town and the Montaña Roja is one of the world's top 10 venues for the sport. The Playa Sur Tenerife Hotel hires boards and is one

Seeing dolphins in the wild is an amazing experience

of the main places to hang out (see page 139). Other good windsurfing spots include the beaches Playa El Cabezo and La Jaquita.

## SPECTATOR SPORTS

### Football

Club Deportivo Tenerife – the *blanquiazules* (blue and whites) – is the main football team, playing at the Heliodoro Rodriguez Lopez Stadium in Santa Cruz, generally on Sunday afternoons.

### Canary wrestling

*Lucha Canaria* is a popular island sport which takes place in village halls and special *terreros* all round the country. It is played on a league basis, in which teams of 12 wrestlers fight individual bouts *(bregas)* in sand rings 10m (33ft) in diameter. The object is to force any part of your opponent's body to the floor using whatever means you can. Exhibition bouts are often staged as part of local fiestas when *juego de palo* or *banot*, a traditional stick-fight, is frequently also held.

## FOR CHILDREN

The island's beaches and salt water pools are a great place for children to while away many an hour, though there is no perceptible tide and the land disappears into the depths very quickly. This means that there is little sea life in the rockpools and on the beaches.

The resorts are well supplied with play parks, rides, zoos and gardens. The Thai-themed waterpark, **Siam Park**

Acrobatics at Loro Parque

(see page 73) and **Loro Parque** (see page 44) are big days out. **Aqualand** in Costa Adeje is a water-park with swimming pools, water slides and a dolphinarium. Free transport is provided from both Playa de las Americas and Los Cristianos. **Jungle Park** near Los Cristianos is a favourite for its exotic bird shows, crocodiles and tigers, set

A Jungle Park gorilla

amid tropical gardens. In Valle de Orotava, **Pueblochico** is a model village of outdoor doll's-house-sized Canarian buildings with botanic gardens and dragon trees in miniature. The **Museo de la Ciencia y el Cosmos** (see page 38) in La Laguna is a hands-on museum with lots of interest for children, as is the **Museo de la Naturaleza y el Hombre** in Santa Cruz (see page 31). Whale- and dolphin-watching trips, as well as visits to the Parque Nacional del Teide, are likely to appeal to all ages.

## SHOPPING

Many **designer shops** have outlets in the big resorts, but there is home-grown talent, too. Spain is known for its well-made and inexpensive **leather goods**, ranging from bags and belts to jackets and coats. Shoes in particular are relatively inexpensive and well designed.

**Embroidery** and **lace-making** are traditional island crafts. Tablecloths and cushion covers with detailed patterns are a speciality. It is best to buy from a shop, such as the Casa de los Balcones in La Orotava, or one of its six branches,

## At the market

Bargaining is expected in the flea markets and at street-side stalls run by the North African merchants, but beware of 'special offers' from these traders, whose goods may include ivory jewellery or leather or fur goods from endangered species. Not only will you be supporting the killing of rare animals, but importing such items into Europe and the US is subject to heavy penalties.

rather than from a street seller, whose goods are often made in Taiwan.

Island **craft** speciality shops include Artenerife (www.artenerife.com), which has several outlets across the island, including one in Casa de la Aduana in Puerto de la Cruz, and one in Casa Torrehermosa in La Orotava. Lava rock and obsidian is used in **sculptures** and a variety of **ceramics** are on sale. Pots are generally plain earthenware, many made in Guanche fashion. There are also copies of their fertility goddesses and die-stamps. At Los Calados in La Laguna (www.loscalados.es) you can purchase Canarian costumes.

**Silver** jewellery is worth looking at and **pearl** shops are a speciality. Tenerife Pearl (www.tenerifepearl.com) has four outlets and a main building with an exhibition at Armeñime on the main road between Adeje and Los Gigantes.

**Cigars**, hand-rolled from local tobacco, are also a good buy. Souvenirs include 50cm-long giant ones. Fancy cigarettes are available too, in pastel colours and prettily boxed. Volcanic gravel impregnated with perfume is a novelty – roll the cigar in it before smoking to sweeten the aroma of the fumes.

Local **wines**, hard to find abroad, make good souvenirs. A good place to buy these from is the Casa del Vino La Baranda at El Sauzal. Tenerife **honey** (*miel*) comes in various guises; there are handmade signs for it along the roadside. The best is from Las Cañadas del Teide – from bees that suck the nectar of Teide broom. Find out all about the different kinds in the Casa de la Miel by the Casa del Vino in El Sauzel. Other groceries to bring home might include jars of red or green *mojo* (see page 99), *bienmesabe* (see page 100) or cactus, papaya and other exotic preserves.

## NIGHTLIFE

Much of Tenerife's nightlife takes place on the streets. There are often spontaneous gatherings in the squares and on the beaches, and music spills out onto the pavements from bars. Holidaymakers can join in the general mood of relaxation.

A typical Canarian traditional costume

In tourist hotspots there are plenty of nightclubs and discos, as well as concerts. Little of the activity starts before midnight. As might be expected, **Playa de las Américas** has the most lavish nightlife on the island. Veronica's is the best known strip, with around 100 bars and discos that keep going until dawn. Some of the most extravagant shows are at Pirámide de Arona, Avenida de las Américas (tel: 922 757 549).

The Santa Cruz Carnaval is one of the most lavish in Europe

The Castillo San Miguel (www.castillosanmiguel.com; tel: 922 700 276), signposted off the *autopista sur* at San Miguel, has medieval nights. In **Costa Adeje** El Faro Chill Art, in the shape of a boat, is a stylish venue with live bands, DJs and a Zen terrace for watching the sunset.

In **Puerto de la Cruz**, Azúcar (Calle Obispo Pérez Cáceres) buzzes with latin beats and locals showing off their salsa skills. Café de Paris at Avenida de Colón is a restaurant with dancing that attracts a slightly older crowd. Head for **Santa Cruz** for vibrant Spanish nightlife or hip bars in the Noria district. **La Laguna** has a busy and varied nightlife scene thanks to its large student population.

The **Auditorio de Tenerife** (www.auditoriodetenerife. com) in Santa Cruz is the home of the admired Orchestra Sinfónica de Tenerife, whose concerts run from the beginning of September until the end of July. It is also the main venue for the island's opera and dance.

# FESTIVALS

Fiestas are a part of island life, and there is a fair chance of catching one during any stay – 30 days a year are officially set aside for festivals, based on the church calendar (see page 97).

## Carnaval

Undoubtedly the most spectacular festival is the pre-Lent carnival. Puerto de la Cruz and Santa Cruz are both overtaken by the event, which is said to rival Rio. Fired by a Latin American fervour, it requires the same great lengths of preparation. Events last for nearly two weeks, starting with the election of a Carnival Queen and climaxing on Shrove Tuesday with the *coso*, the grand parade, with floats on various themes, and everyone in the fanciest carnival dress. There is a strong transvestite element and dancers are accompanied by *murgas*, groups singing satirical songs. The event draws to a close on Ash Wednesday with El Entierro de la Sardina (the burial of the sardine), a mock funeral attended by people in outrageous outfits, who beat their breasts and shed crocodile tears.

## Where to gamble

Casino Puerto de la Cruz (Avenida Cristóbal Colón 1, Puerto de la Cruz, www.casinostenerife.com; tel: 922 368 843) is probably one of the best casinos in Europe. Other casinos include Casino Santa Cruz (Rambla de Santa Cruz 105; Santa Cruz de Tenerife, tel: 922 824 060) and Casino Playa de las Américas (Av. Rafael Puig LLuvina, Adeje, tel: 922 793 758),

You will need your passport for entry to the casinos. Find more details at www.casinostenerife.com.

Local fiesta, local dress

## Corpus Christi

One of the most widely celebrated religous festivals on the island is the eight days (Octavo) of Corpus Christi at the end of May or the beginning of June. The best places to see it celebrated are La Laguna and La Orotava, where pavements are covered with spectacular carpets made out of flowers and a wide array of colours from volcanic sand. The procession that makes its way over them crushes the flower petals and fills the air with their scent.

## Romerías

Corpus Christi marks the beginning of the Romería season of local festivals involving food, wine and dancing. Again it is La Orotava and La Laguna that put on the biggest shows, with, respectively, the Romería de San Isidro in mid-June and the Romería de San Benita a fortnight later. Arico, Granadilla, Güímar and Icod also have large Romerías during the month.

## Assumption

The biggest pilgrimage takes place on the day of the Assumption (15 August) at Candelaria, where the statue of Our Lady of Candelaria, patron saint of the Canary Islands, is paraded in the streets. On the day before there is a re-enactment of the appearance of the Virgin to the Guanche shepherds.

# Festivals

For public holidays, see page 124.

**January:** *Cabalgata de los Reyes* (Procession of the Three Kings, Santa Cruz and Garachico), with costumes, brass bands and camel cavalcades.

**February/March:** *Carnaval*, Santa Cruz's extravaganza; also in Puerto de la Cruz.

**March/April:** *Semana Santa* (Holy Week): solemn pre-Easter processions in many towns and cities throughout the island.

**April:** local fiestas on 25th (Icod, Tegueste).

**May:** spring festivals, opera festival (Santa Cruz). Fiestas de la Cruz (all places with Cruz [cross] in their name): processions, festivities and fireworks. Festival of San Isidro and Santa María de la Cabeza (Los Realejos and La Orotava) with large firework display.

*Fiesta de Corpus Christi* (late May or early June, in La Laguna, La Orotava and elsewhere): beautiful flower carpets.

**June:** *Romería de San Isidro* (Tacoronte), *Romería de San Benito* (La Laguna): ox-drawn carts laden with local produce. Local fiestas (Arico, El Sauzal, Granadilla, Güímar, Icod).

**July:** *Fiesta de la Virgen del Carmen*, patron saint of seamen. *Romerías de Santiago Apóstol* (Festival of St James, Santa Cruz): pilgrimage, fireworks. Local fiestas (Candelaria, La Laguna, Los Realojos, Santiago del Teide).

**August:** *Fiesta de la Asunción* (Assumption, Candelaria): re-enactment of the appearance of the Blessed Virgin to the Guanches. Local fiestas (Garachico, Los Cristianos).

**September:** *Fiestas del Santísimo Cristo* (La Laguna, Tacoronte): floats, fireworks, sports, theatre and poetry. Local festivals (Güímar, Guía de Isora). *Fiestas de Nuestra Señora de las Mercedes de Rojas* (El Médano in Granadilla): honours patron saint. Grape harvest.

**October:** Local fiesta (Granadilla).
Wine tasting festival in Icod, La Orotava and Puerto de la Cruz.

**November:** Fiesta de San Andrés (also known as La Fiesta del Cacharro y la Castaña), Puerto de la Cruz.

**December:** *Navidad* (Christmas). *Noche Vieja* (New Year's Eve).

# EATING OUT

There is no shortage of restaurants serving chicken and pizza in the resorts, and Chinese restaurants are a popular alternative for *tinerfeños*. But any visitor should concentrate on getting to know the local dishes, which are the staple of most restaurants across the island. These are based on home-grown pulses and vegetables, fish from the Atlantic, and meat from indigenous animals. Portions are generally healthy, and establishments are usually relaxed, so you can be as picky as you like. *Cocina Canario*, *cocina casa linga* and *típico* are signs of local cooking. *Tapas*, small dishes to eat as appetisers, are served in many bars and restaurants and they can be made into a meal. There are also eminently palatable wines from the island's five recognised denominated regions.

Tapas topped with red and white fish, lemon and parsley

# WHAT TO EAT

## Vegetables

Potatoes are one of the mainstays of the island, and the fact that they are called *papas* here, as they are in South America, and not *patatas*, as they are in Spain, is a clue to their affinities. There are no blights known to the local tuber, and there are a dozen

Papas arrugadas

regularly grown Andean varieties, notably *papa negra*, black potatoes. The size of squash balls and the colour of wood ash, they are usually prepared *arrugadas* or 'wrinkled', boiled in their jackets in highly salted water (traditionally sea water) and usually served with a *mojo* sauce.

*Mojo* sauces, to accompany both fish and meat dishes, are made of olive oil, herbs and spices and come in two colours – red and green. These are either poured on to a dish or served in their own bowls for you to dip into or spoon out. Restaurants have their own recipes. The red *mojo picón* has dried peppers, chilli or paprika; the green *mojo verde* is made of parsley or, more distinctly, coriander (*cilantro*).

Sweet potatoes, or yams, are also grown and can be seen piled high in the markets, but they are by and large absent from restaurant menus.

Another Latin American influence is corn cobs (*piñas de millo*), used widely in soups and stews including the traditional *puchero canario*, in which a variety of local vegetables and pulses are likely to appear, such as chickpeas (*gabanzos*), kidney beans and *bubango*, a particular kind of marrow.

A typical Canarian roasted sea fish

Soups are plentiful and include *vieja ropa* ('old clothes'), a kind of minestrone into which anything goes, and rancho *canario*, a watercress soup.

Salad ingredients are generally fresh and tomatoes are particularly tasty.

## Gofio

Wherever you eat on the island, it won't be long before you encounter *gofio*, the staple food of the Guanche. This is toasted ground corn, generally maize, but sometimes barley or wheat or even chickpeas, and it is served in a variety of ways. It can be added to soups as a thickener, and it comes as a seasoned broth, *escaldon*, usually served in an earthenware dish. It is also used as an accompaniment to dishes, or as a dessert, when it is made into a milk pudding *(frangollo)* or a mousse *(mus)* served with *bienmesabe* ('it tastes good to me') made from almonds and honey.

## Meat

Tenerife is not a great meat-eating land. There is beef and pork, but the principal interest lies in local goat *(cabrito)*, usually simply grilled, and rabbit *(conejo)*. *Conejo en salmorejo* is a stew of diced rabbit in a marinade, which is fried and boiled in its own juices and may be served with *papas arrugadas*. *Costillas con papas de piñas de millo* is a stew of pork ribs, potatoes and corn cobs.

## Fish

Fish is the glory of the island. The deep cold surrounding waters produce meaty flesh with a lot of flavour. Even sardines, simply grilled, are delicious. Parrot fish *(vieja)* have such delicate scales that they are not cleaned for cooking, and you have to skim them off on your plate, moving the knife up from the tail. In fresh fish restaurants larger fish is often sold by the kilo, in which case you will find that white fish *(blanco)* is slightly more expensive than oily fish *(azul)*. There are local mussels *(lapas)*, and the large prawns *(gambas)* make an excellent *tapa*.

### Fish on the menu

Many of the exotic Atlantic fish you will see on the extensive menus in Tenerife are unlike any you will see in most of Spain, and some are not easily translated. These include:

*Abadejo* – pollack; *aguja azul* – blue marlin; *bacalao* – cod; *chipirón* – baby squid; *caballa* – horse mackerel; *cabrilla* – grouper; *cherne* – sea bass; *choco* – cuttlefish; *congrio* – conger eel; *burro* – donkey fish; *corvino* – corb; *dorado* – gilthead bream; *lenguado* – sole; *merluza* – hake; *mero* – grouper; *morena* – moray eel; *pez espada* – sword fish; *rodaballo* – turbot; *salema* – gold-lined bream; *salmoneta* – red mullet; *same* – gold bream; *sarda* – mackerel; *sargo* – white bream; *vieja* – parrot fish.

Ronmiel, the local rum

A *cazuelo* (stew) of fish is a good way to sample what is available. This is made with a wide variety of fish in recognisable chunks, with some vegetables added. Portions are generous.

## Fruit

The island's exotic fruits arrive on the table whole or in juice drinks. Bananas are mostly of the small Dwarf Cavendish variety, and are sometimes served for breakfast with fried eggs and rice – a Cuban speciality. Interesting fruit to try includes prickly pear, *chirimoya* or custard apples and *níspero*, small yellow medlars that ripen in May. Roadside stalls are one way to find them fresh.

Papaya, mango and prickly pear (cactus) are all abundant and are turned into fruit juices.

## Cheese

There are a number of local cheeses to try, made from both goats' and sheep's milk and varying in strength from mild to tangy. Cheese is not universally available and if you see any advertised on your travels around the island, it is well worth seeking out. Arico, in the island's south, is a cheese-making centre.

## WHERE TO EAT

Good restaurants are to be found along the main roads, as well as in the main towns. *¡Que Bueno!*, a book of top restaurants, is published every year, with text in both Spanish and English, though its entries tend to be skewed towards the swanky establishments of the Costa Adeje.

## Tascas and Bodegas

Tenerife has a tradition of *tascas*, small eating houses where you can also go just for a drink. A number of these have become rather smart in Santa Cruz and elsewhere, with cutting-edge young chefs seeking to make their mark. *Bodegas, bodegones* and *bodeguitas*, originally wine houses, are fairly indistinguishable bars with *tapas* and even full meals provided. Pick what you want from a menu: there is no formality about having to have courses in any particular order, or with any particular accompaniment.

*Tinerfeños* eat lunch, their main meal, around 2 or 3 pm, and dinner from around 9pm. A number of restaurants close on Sunday night and one day a week, often Monday.

Tenerife's fruits are put to good use

## WHAT TO DRINK

### Tea and coffee

There are plenty of places to drop in for a drink. Coffee is the leisure daytime drink of the island. As on mainland Spain, you can have *café* solo (equivalent to an espresso), *cortado* in a glass tumbler with a little milk, *café con leche* with milk and *Americano* or *largo*, a solo with extra water. Occasionally you may be asked if you want a black (*negro*) or brown (*marrón*) roast. Cafés often do deals for breakfasts, including

## Local spirits

Local rum (*ron*) is made from cane sugar. Sweet liqueurs include *ronmiel*, made from palm sap, and *cobana*, made from bananas.

juice and perhaps a roll or croissant. Cakes and pastries are usually on offer, but away from the main towns fresh bread is not always available until later in the day. Tea is generally a bag in hot water, usually taken as a remedy for stomach aches.

Fresh orange and other juices are usually available and the local beer, Dorada, is a blond lager that will quench any thirst.

## Wine

Tenerife is the main wine-making Canary Island. Although it produces around 5 million litres a year, there is no guarantee that a local label will be on your restaurant wine list. Because of tourist demand there is not enough of the local wine to go round, and you frequently find that prices of Tenerife wine are higher than those of bottles from mainland Spain.

The island is divided into five *Denominaciónes de Origen* (DO), and because of the great difference in altitude, the grape harvest is staggered. If you are here on 29 November, the eve of St Andrew's day, make for the wine-tasting festivals in La Orotava, Puerto de la Cruz and, most entertainingly, Icod de los Vinos, where people slide on boards down the cobbled streets and make a racket with tin cans, echoing the old barrel runs down to the former port.

The **Abona** do region in the south reaches right up to Vilaflor, making the vineyards about the highest in the world. They produce mainly white wines from a dozen grape varieties, plus a few reds and rosés.

**Valle de la Orotava** covers the municipalities of La Orotava, Realejos and Puerto de la Cruz, and produces full reds and whites.

**Tacoronte-Acentejo** is the best known and most productive of the regions. Brands include Viña Norte and Humboldt Tinto. The Tacoronte-Acentejo wine route offers guided or self-guided tours to wineries, restaurants and places of interest in the region. Check www.enotenerife.com for more wine routes. **Ycoden-Daute-Isora** has a long history of producing light, aromatic reds as well as whites.

**Valle de Güímar** produces white wines from grapes including the Gual and Verdella, grown between 600 and 800m (2,000–2,600ft).

There is also a substantial amount of fortified wine made from Malvasía or muscatel grapes. Wineries *(bodegas)* are generally places where you can just drop in, and if you book ahead, some will show you around. The best place to find out about the island's wines is the Casa del Vino La Baranda (see page 109, or visit www.casadelvinotenerife.com).

Wine in traditional bottles

## TO HELP YOU ORDER

Could we have a table? **¿Nos puede dar una mesa, por favor?**

Do you have a set menu? **¿Tiene un menú del día?**

I would like... **Quisiera...**

The bill, please **La cuenta, por favour**

## MENU READER

**agua minerale** mineral water

**à la plancha** grilled

**al ajillo** in garlic

**al punto** medium

**arroz** rice

**asado** roast

**atún** tuna

**azúcar** sugar

**bacalao** cod

**bocadillo** sandwich

**boquerones** anchovies

**buen hecho** well done

**buey/res** beef

**café** coffee

**calamares** squid

**cangrejo** crab

**cerdo** pork

**cerveza** beer

**champiñones** mushrooms

**chorizo** spicy sausage

**cocido** stew

**cordero** lamb

**ensalada** salad

**entremeses** hors-d'oeuvre

**helado** ice cream

**jamón serrano** cured ham

**judías** beans

**langosta** lobster

**leche** milk

**mariscos** shellfish

**mejillones** mussels

**pan** bread

**pescado** fish

**picante** spicy

**poco hecho** rare

**pollo** chicken

**postre** dessert

**pulpitos** baby octopus

**queso** cheese

**sal** salt

**ternera** veal

**tortilla** omelette

**trucha** trout

**salsa** sauce

**vino** wine

**verduras** vegetables

# PLACES TO EAT

*We have used the following symbols to give an idea of the price for a three-course meal for one, including wine, cover and service:*

**€€€€** over 50 euros       **€€** 25–40 euros

**€€€** 40–50 euros       **€** under 25 euros

## THE NORTHEAST

## ANAGA

**Cruz del Carmen €** *Las Mercedes Km6, tel: 922 25 00 62.* An ideal stop, by the Cruz del Carmen mirador, when exploring the Anaga Hills. Good solid Canarian cooking, with both meat and fish soups and home-made sweets, in three spacious dining rooms.

## SAN CRISTOBAL DE LA LAGUNA

**Herradores 18 €€** *Calle Herradores 18, tel: 922 25 52 81.* A perfect place for a night out with friends. Tapas as well as main dishes are equally delicious. Good choice of wines and excellent service.

**Restaurante Santo Domingo €€** *Calle Santo Domingo 24, tel: 922 10 12 12.* A tasca known for its selection of hams and cheeses, as well as meats and seafood, including delicious octopus. Good local wines at moderate prices.

**Tasca la Comarca €€** *Camino de San Bartolome de Geneto 95, tel: 922 31 12 46.* This small restaurant and bar serves excellent food including a wide selection of *tapas* typical for the Spanish region of Asturias. Make sure you leave space (and the portions are big) for a dessert, *arroz con leche* is excellent. Good service.

## LOS NARANJEROS

**Restaurante El Empedrado €€** *Carretera General del Norte 284, tel: 922 56 74 35,* www.empedrado.es. Set in an old house, this is one of many popular restaurants between La Laguna and Tacoronte that fill up with diners at weekend lunchtimes. The house speciality is grilled meat offered in plentiful supply: chicken, pork, veal, rabbit, lamb, goat, but the *cochino negro canario* is particularly recommended. The wine and desserts are also good. Good value for money.

## SANTA CRUZ

**El Aguila €€** *Plaza Alféreces Provisionales, tel: 922 27 31 56*. This restaurant is set in a central pedestrian square with plenty to watch – including a large screen outside when a big football game is on. Has an extensive selection of *tapas* with large *parillas* of fish or meat – go to the counter and point to the ones that take your fancy.

**El Gusto por el Vino €** *Av. San Sebastían 51, Mercado La Recova, Santa Cruz*, www.elgustoporelvino.com. A restaurant and a wine-bar with *tapas* opened by the biggest local wine distributor in a popular market La Recova. Short but tasty menu.

**Gastrobar MNH Armando Saldanha €€** *Calle Fuente Morales s/n, Santa Cruz, tel: 922 083 043*, www.museosdetenerife. org. A small cafeteria in the Museo de la Naturaleza y El Hombre opened by the acclaimed Mexican chef Armando Saldanha. Famous for his *tapas*.

**La Hierbita €€** *Calle El Clavel 19, tel: 922 24 46 17*, www.la hierbita.com. Located in a delightful old house with several small rooms spread across two floors, the restaurant serves home-made cuisine from popular Canarian recipes. *Try alma-grote gomero*, a rich cheese from La Gomera, Canarian stew or grilled fish and end with home-made dessert and La Hierbita, a traditional liqueur.

**La Posada del Pez €€** *Carretera Taganana 2, San Andrés, tel: 922 591 948*. A small, but excellent seafood restaurant near the Playa de las Teresitas. *A mar y montaña* (sea and montain), which is a mix of fish and oxtail in one plate, is worth a try. Sunday closed for dinner.

**Taberna Ramon €€** *Rambla de Santa Cruz, 56, tel: 922 24 13 67.* A typical *taberna* with good ambience, *horror vacui* décor and pork legs hanging from the ceiling. You are spoiled for choice of a tempting array of *tapas* and scores of different wines.

## THE NORTH

## EL SAUZAL

**Casa del Vino La Baranda €€€** *Autopista General del Norte Km21, tel: 922 57 25 35,* www.casadelvinotenerife.com. The restaurant in this elegant 17th-century estate, now occupied by the wine museum, serves good modern Canarian food, and is the best place to try – and seek advice about – Canarian wines. There is also a tasca bar that has views from the terrace down to the sea. Closed on Mondays.

**Restaurante Casa Odon €€** *Carretera General del Norte km 21, tel: 922 56 11 24,* http://restaurantecasaodon.com. Good-value restaurant dedicated to authentic Canarian cuisine. The portions are abundant and delicious and the service is quick and efficient. The mushroom plates are recommended.

## ICOD DE LOS VINOS

**El Mortero €€** *Camino Guayadil 1, tel: 922 81 49 55,* www.restauranteelmortero.com. The food in this restaurant is creative, abundant and good quality. The traditional menu changes every six months and is based on seasonal products. A bit pricey, but definitely worth a try.

## LA OROTAVA

**El Engazo €€** *Ctra. Antigua la Luz. Las Candias, tel: 922 33 35 56.* The *finca* of the Pontes Mendéz estate was bought by the chef Manuel Luis Dominguez in 1963, since when it has acquired a reputation for friendliness and good local dishes. Now, the new owners, in a new location, on the other side of the road, continue the tradition. The octopus stew is exceptional. The good-quality food is accompanied by beautiful views.

**Lucas Maes €€€€** *Barranco La Arena 53, tel: 922 32 11 59,* www.restaurantelucasmaes.com. Named after the chef, this is an old colonial-style house where you can tuck into mouth-watering fusion fare and enjoy views from the terraces and gardens. Tenerife-born Lucas Maes was trained in Belgium and France and is regarded as one of the island's best chefs. Everything, down to the breadsticks, is made on the premises. Closed Sunday and Monday.

**Sabor Canario €€** *Calle Carrera Escultor Estevez 17, tel: 922 32 27 93,* http://hotelruralorotava.es. This old townhouse in La Orotava's historic centre dates from 1580. The dishes are traditional too, including rabbit in *solmerejo* sauce, and various manifestations of *gofio* (roasted barley flour). It also has a good selection of wines.

**Victoria €–€€** *Hermano Apolinar 8, tel: 922 33 16 83,* www.hotel ruralvictoria.com. This restaurant is beautifully located on an indoor patio at the heart of La Orotava's old town. Daily fix-price and good value menu for €10.50, which includes a starter, main plate, dessert and glass of wine (beer or water are other options). Once a month there is a special thematic menu prepared by award-wining chef Richard Etherington.

## PUERTO DE LA CRUZ

**Restaurante La Carta €€€** *Calle San Felipe 53, tel: 922 38 15 92.* This small, popular restaurant offers good ambience, friendly service and a creative menu. Tuna carpaccio is excellent. There is also a selection of vegetarian dishes. Closed Wednesdays.

**La Gañaninía €€€** *Camino El Durazno 71, tel: 922 37 10 00,* www. laganania.com. Located up towards the motorway near the Abaco museum-house, this is the converted stable of an 18th-century farmhouse, which has wonderful views over Puerto de la Cruz. The menu is Canarian, with *tapas* dishes.

**Meson El Monasterio €€** *La Montañeta, Los Realejos, tel: 922 34 07 07*, www.mesonelmonasterio.com. This former monastery enjoys stunning views from its terraces and gardens. Four different restaurants cater for all tastes, whether it's *carnes a la piedra* (meat cooked on stone), seafood specialities, Canarian and Spanish cuisine, international haute cuisine or just a plate of *tapas*. The Bodega has a wide selection of wines, and the on-site shop stocks hams, salami, olives and cheeses.

**El Oriental €€€** *Avenida Richard J. Yeoward, tel: 922 38 14 00*, https://hotelbotanico.com. Located within the Hotel Botánico (see page 137), the speciality is Thai cookery with pan-Asiatic touches. The ambiance here is formal and the cuisine is enticing. Open for dinner Thursday–Monday. Closed in June.

**Régulo €€€** *Calle Pérez Zamora 16, tel: 922 38 45 06*, www.restauranteregulo.com. One of the best restaurants in Puerto de la Cruz, Régulo occupies a typical Canarian 18th-century house with balconies around a delightful patio. Specialities of the house include *lapas a la plancha* (grilled limpet shells) and *solomillo relleno de camembert* (fillet steak with camembert stuffing). Open for lunch and dinner, closed Sunday, and Monday lunchtime.

**La Rosa di Bari €€** *Calle El Lomo 23, tel: 922 36 85 23*. This popular Italian restaurant is set in a small, tastefully decorated house in La Ranilla, Puerto de La Cruz's fisherman's quarter. Dishes on offer include a number of unique reworking of traditional Italian favourites. The fresh pastas and seafood dishes are particularly good. Closed September.

## TEGUESTE

**Casa Tomás €€** *Camino del Portezuelo 2, tel: 922 63 80 07*, www.restaurante-bodegoncasatomas.es. Home-made Canarian food, with dishes including spare ribs with potatoes and chickpea stews. Busy at weekends. Closed on Mondays

## THE NORTHWEST

### GARACHICO

**Anturium in Hotel San Roque €€€** *Calle Esteban de Ponte 32, Garachico, tel: 922 133 435*, http://hotelsanroque.com. It offers a mix of Canarian and Mediterranean cuisines with delicacies such as *dorada en sal* (bream baked in rock salt) and *paella duo* (with squid). Great selection of wines.

### GAÍA DE ISORA

**M.B. €€€€** *Abama Gran Hotel and Resort, tel: 922 12 60 00*, www.ritzcarlton.com. The signature restaurant of the Basque chef, Martin Berasategui (hence the name), renowned for inspirational Mediterranean cuisine. The restaurant has gained a Michelin star so expect gourmet fare.

### MASCA

**La Pimentera €€€** *tel: 922  86 34 38*. A delightful setting, looking down over the Barranco, with a shady terrace full of flowers. Serves good local food prepared with organic fruits and vegetables from its own garden. The desserts are delicious.

## THE SOUTH

### CHAYOFA

**La Finca del Arte €€** *Calle Centro 1, tel: 922 72 91 03*, www.fincadelarte.com. Situated between Playa de las Américas and Arona, this former tomato packing factory functions as an art gallery for local talent as well as a café and bistro. Good to drop in to any time of day; it livens up on Sundays with a jazz brunch.

### LA CALETA

**Masía del Mar €€** *El Muelle 3, tel: 922 71 08 95*. This great harbourside fish restaurant offers a real flavour of the Tenerife coast. Set in a restored warehouse dating from 1568, it serves some of the freshest fish and the most authentic dishes available on the coast.

## LOS ABRIGOS

**Restaurante Los Abrigos €€€** *Paseo Maritimo, tel: 922 17 02 64,* www.restaurantelosabrigos.com. Wonderful port-side restaurant with extensive menu of fish, from *abadejo* (pollack) to *vieja* (parrot fish). Crowded at weekends. Closed Wednesdays, but the next door Perlas de Mar has a similarly serious fish menu.

**Los Roques €€€** *Calle la Marina, tel: 922 74 94 01* www. restaurantelosroques.com. One of the more sophisticated seafood restaurants lining the seafront, where you can try local smoked ostrich with foie grasterrine, as well as freshly caught Dorada, king prawns or seafood terrine. Offers good tasting menus. Reserve a table alfresco to make the most of the sunset. Closed Sunday lunch and all day on Monday.

## LOS CRISTIANOS

**Chez Jacques €€€** *Paseo Roma s/n, Los Cristianos, tel: 922 790 569.* Opened in 1974, it's one of the oldest restaurants on the island, serving classic French fare including a superb beef Bourguignon with six homemade sauces to choose from. Open for dinner only. Closed on Mon.

**Habibi €€** *Avenida De La Habana, San Telmo, tel: 922 75 09 51.* Tourists enjoy this cheap and cheerful touch of Lebanon on the island. Offers great views, especially at the sunset and delicious food. The service is also very efficient.

## PLAYA DE LAS AMÉRICAS

**Molino Blanco €€€€** *Avenida Austria 5, tel: 922 79 62 82,* www. molino-blanco.com. Charcoal grills and wood-fired ovens are the keynote of this well-known restaurant, which has such delights as suckling pig (*cochinillo*), ostrich (*avastruz*), hare (*ciervo*) and boar (*jabalí*) as well as fresh fish. It has an animated atmosphere in its three dining rooms, with live music, and the landmark white windmill makes it easy to find.

**First Love €€** *Paseo Tarajal, Centro Commercial Compostela Beach, tel: 635 89 22 30.* This small, unpretentious Italian restaurant is a little gem serving homemade pasta dishes. The friendly owners make the meal even more enjoyable. The menu with Italian classics is rather short, but also features good salads. Highly recommended.

**La Tasca €€€** *Gran Hotel Bahia del Duque, Avenida Bruselas s/n, tel: 922 74 69 32,* www.bahia-duque.com. A Spanish restaurant in décor, style and cuisine, with staff in traditional costume. The menu is a mix of familiar and unusual dishes, and there is live music with flamenco guitar.

**Mesón Las Lanzas €€€€** *Avenida Noelia Afonso Cabrera, Res. Las Viñas, 8, tel: 922 79 11 72,* www.mesonlaslanzas.es. It's not easy to find a restaurant serving Spanish food in this very touristic part of the island. This one is rather expensive, but worth paying for. The décor is traditional Spanish and so is the menu. Great choice of seafood and excellent wines.

## SAN ISIDRO

**Mesón de Antonio €€** *Cuevas de cho portada, tel: 922 39 02 72.* This nice restaurant, located just off the town, offers excellent meat dishes. Great desserts and service. Closed Tuesdays.

## THE SOUTHWEST

## ADEJE

**Otelo 1 €€** *Calle Los Molinos, Barranco del Infierno, tel: 922 78 03 74,* www.restauranteotelo1tf.com. At the entrance of the dramatic Barranco del Infierno gorge, this unpretentious bar/restaurant is popular with hikers. The main dishes are rabbit or crispy garlic chicken, preferably washed down with local wine. Closed Tuesday.

# A–Z TRAVEL TIPS

A Summary of Practical Information

A Accommodation . . . 116
  Airports. . . . . . . . . . . . 117
B Bicycle Rental . . . . . . 117
  Budgeting for
    Your Trip . . . . . . . . 117
C Camping . . . . . . . . . . 118
  Car hire . . . . . . . . . . . 118
  Climate . . . . . . . . . . . 119
  Clothing. . . . . . . . . . . 119
  Crime. . . . . . . . . . . . . 120
  Customs and Entry
    Requirements . . . 120
D Driving. . . . . . . . . . . . 120
E Electricity. . . . . . . . . . 121
  Embassies and
    Consulates . . . . . . 122
  Emergencies. . . . . . . . 122
G Gay and Lesbian
    Travellers. . . . . . . . 123
  Getting to
    Tenerife. . . . . . . . . 123

H Health and
    Medical Care . . . . 123
  Holidays . . . . . . . . . . . 124
L Language . . . . . . . . . . 125
  Lost Property . . . . . . 125
M Maps. . . . . . . . . . . . . 126
  Media. . . . . . . . . . . . . 126
  Money Matters. . . . . 126
O Opening Hours . . . . 127
P Police. . . . . . . . . . . . . 128
  Post Offices . . . . . . . . 128
  Public Transport. . . . 128
T Taxis . . . . . . . . . . . . . 129
  Telephones . . . . . . . . 130
  Time Differences. . . 131
  Tipping . . . . . . . . . . . 131
  Toilets. . . . . . . . . . . . 131
  Tourist Information 131
  Travellers with
    Disabilities. . . . . . . 133
W Websites . . . . . . . . . . 133

# A

## ACCOMMODATION

Most hotels and apartments are concentrated in the main towns and resorts, particularly in the south of the island. The standard of accommodation is generally high, with a large number of luxury resort hotels. Styles vary from contemporary design to traditional Canarian houses, country houses (*casas rurales*) to country estates (*fincas*). Package tourism predominates but recent years have seen a growing number of hotels for independent travellers, especially in the quieter north. Prices are reasonable by EU standards and establishments are graded from one-star to five-star Gran Lujo (GL) which signifies top-of-the-range quality, but stars are not always directly reflected in the price. Santa Cruz de Tenerife and Puerto de la Cruz have a selection of lower-rated places. By law, prices must be displayed in hotel reception areas and in the rooms. Breakfast is not always included in the basic rate.

There are plenty of apartments, which are graded with one to three 'keys', shown with symbols, depending on their amenities. There are also 'aparthotels', often graded as hotels, where each room or suite has its own kitchen facilities yet retains all the trappings of a hotel.

If you are visiting during the more expensive high season (December, July and August), book accomodation well in advance and be aware that minimum stays in some hotels are 3–5 days. The official Tenerife website, www.webtenerife.com, gives details of around 200 places to stay; for country houses visit www.ecoturismocanarias.com.

a single/double room with bath/shower **una habitación individual/doble con baño/ducha**
What's the rate per night? **¿Cuál es el precio por noche?**
Is breakfast included? **¿Está incluído el desayuno?**

## AIRPORTS *(aeropuertos)*

There are two airports on the island. Most international flights use Reina Sofía Airport (Tenerife Sur) in the south (tel: 902 404 704) at Granadilla de Abona, 11 miles (18km) east of Los Cristianos. Buses run to Los Cristianos and Playa de las Américas (about 25 minutes) and to Puerto de la Cruz, (1hr 40 min). Los Rodeos Airport (Tenerife Norte) near La Laguna (tel: 902 404 704/922 553 700) handles mainly inter-island and Spanish air traffic. For general airport information, see www.aena.es.

## B

## BICYCLE RENTAL

Cycling is a good way of seeing the island but be prepared for hot and challenging rides in the mountainous areas. CA Cycling Tenerife (www.clubactivocycling.com, tel: 669 624 373) offers cycling tours for all levels of fitness, cycling packages with accommodation and bike hire for individuals. See also page 84 for Rafting Bike. Bike Point Tenerife (www.bikepointtenerife.com) is a bike shop that also rents bikes and offers cycling tours.

## BUDGETING FOR YOUR TRIP

Here's a list of some average prices in euros.

**Accommodation:** Rates for a double room can range from as low as €35 at a *pensión* or *hostal* to as much as €400 at a top-of-the-range five-star hotel. A pleasant three-star hotel will cost in the range of €90–€100. However, rates increase during the high season, beginning around late November and culminating with the Carnaval in February/March.

**Apartments:** For a family apartment prices per night range from around €30 for one key to more than €80 for three keys. Discounts are often available for longer stays.

**Attractions:** Most museums and gardens charge a minimal entry fee of around €5. More expensive (€10–30) are the larger attractions such as the Pirámides de Güímar and theme parks such as Loro Parque.

**Car hire:** Around €35 a day.

**Meals and drinks:** In a bar, a continental breakfast will cost from €4. The cheapest three-course meal, *menú del día*, with one drink, in a small bar/restaurant, will be around €8. Dinner in a medium level restaurant will be €25–€30 per person, including wine.

**Petrol:** Around €0.90 a litre.

**Sports:** Golf green fees (per day) range from €45–85 for 18 holes. Tennis court fees start at about €6 an hour, and horse riding starts at about €20 an hour.

**Taxis:** A taxi journey within a town is likely to cost €4–5. The fare from Playa de las Américas to Reina Sofía airport is around €36.

## C

### CAMPING

Camping is not a common option on the island, and it is prohibited in the national parks. There is a site on the south coast, Camping Nauta Cañada Blanca, in Las Galletas, 2km (1 mile) from the beach (tel: 922 78 51 18). Two other camping sites are Punta del Hidalgo (tel: 922 60 11 00) in La Laguna and Quimpi (tel: 922 69 03 33; www. quimpi.com) in El Rosario.

### CAR HIRE *(coches de alquiler)* (see also Driving)

Usually you must be over 21, sometimes 24, to rent a car, and you will need your passport, a major credit card and a valid driving licence that you have held for at least 12 months. Cars are generally manual transmission.

There are around 100 local car-hire companies – 25 in Santa Cruz alone – and these tend to be cheaper than the better known companies. It is also cheaper if you hire a car before you leave home, especially online. Local companies include Amigoautos (www.amigoautos.es), and Tenerife Rent a Car (www.trc-cars.com). All the big international companies (Avis, Europcar, Hertz) have offices at the airports and in the major towns.

> I'd like to rent a car for one day/week. **Quisiera alquilar un coche por un día/una semana.**
> Please include full insurance. **Haga el favor de incluir el seguro a todo riesgo.**

## CLIMATE

With the temperature a fairly steady 22°C (72°F) year-round, sunshine is the rule, but the weather in the north and eastern parts of the island can be changeable. In spring there is a cold and wet gust from the northwest, and in autumn the famous hot sirocco raises temperatures. Remember that the island is on a parallel with West Africa, and the temperatures in the southern resorts and in the *malpaís* can be high. Up in the hills, it becomes much cooler, even in the town of La Laguna, and the trade winds keep the northeast of the island damp for most of the year. Temperatures drop to minus figures around El Teide's snowcapped summit and in the Cañadas.

## CLOTHING

In addition to summer clothes and beachwear, bring a sweater or jacket for evenings. For excursions to high altitudes, you will also need warmer, rainproof clothing and sturdy shoes.

Casual wear is the norm, although in five-star hotels, the best restaurants and the casinos, a jacket and tie, though not obligatory, will not be out of place for men.

Topless bathing is quite common, and is acceptable at most hotel pools. Beachwear, shorts, bikini tops and mini-skirts should not be worn when visiting religious places.

## CRIME

Tenerife does not have a high crime rate and theft is only really likely in tourist areas. There is some opportunistic bag snatching and pick-pocketing in busy places such as markets or at fiestas though. Never leave anything of value in your car and use the safe deposit box in your room for all valuables, including your passport. Burglaries of holiday apartments do occur, so keep doors and windows locked when you are absent. Report all thefts to the local police within 24 hours for your own insurance purposes.

I want to report a theft. **Quiero denunciar un robo.**

## CUSTOMS AND ENTRY REQUIREMENTS

Most visitors, including citizens of all EU countries, the USA, Canada, Australia and New Zealand, require only a valid passport to enter Spain. Although Spain is in the EU, there is still a restriction on duty-free allow-ances at customs (*aduana*) when returning to the UK from the Canary Islands. This is: 200 cigarettes or 50 cigars or 250g smoking tobacco; 1 litre spirits over 22 percent or 2 litres under 22 percent, 2 litres of wine.

## D

## DRIVING

**Driving conditions.** Drive on the right, pass on the left, yield right-of-way to all vehicles coming from your right. Slow down when pass-ing through villages and be aware that you may encounter anything from a herd of goats and donkey and cart, to large potholes.

**Speed limits** on the island are 120 km/h (74mph) on motorways, 100km/h (62mph) on dual highways, 90km/h (52mph) on country roads, 50km/h (31mph) in built-up areas and 20km/h (13mph) in residential areas.

**Motorways** are toll-free. In the main towns traffic can be heavy and one-way systems confusing, as road signs are woefully inadequate.

**Parking.** You are more likely to find a parking space during lunch hours (2–4pm). Consider parking at the edge of towns and taking buses or taxis to the centre.

**Petrol.** Petrol stations on main roads are often open 24 hours and most take credit cards. They are less frequent off the beaten track and often close at night and on Sundays. Most hire cars take unleaded petrol, which in Spain is called *sin plomo*.

**Traffic police.** Civil guards (*Guardia Civil*) patrol the roads on black motorbikes. In towns the municipal police handle traffic control. If you are fined for a traffic offence, you will have to pay on the spot.

**Seat belts** are compulsory. Children under 10 must travel in the rear. Using mobile phones or GPS devices while driving is illegal.

**Road signs.** Apart from the standard international pictographs you may encounter the following:

**Aparcamiento** Parking
**Desviación** Detour
**Obras** Road works
**Peligro** Danger
**Senso unico** One way

**¿Se puede aparcar aqui?** Can I park here?
**Llénelo, por favor, con super**. Fill the tank please, top grade.
**Ha habido un accidente**. There has been an accident.

# E

## ELECTRICITY (*corriente eléctrica*)

The standard supply is 220v with continental-style two-pin sockets. North American 110v appliances will need a transformer.

## EMBASSIES AND CONSULATES *(consulados)*

Santa Cruz de Tenerife: **United Kingdom**: Plaza Weyler, 8, 1st Floor, tel: 928 26 25 08, Mon, Tue and Fri 8.30am–1.30pm. **Republic of Ireland (Honorary Consulate)**: C/ San Francisco nº 9, 1º dcha, tel: 922 24 56 71, Mon–Fri 10am–1pm.

The nearest **US** consulate is in Las Palmas, capital of neighbouring Gran Canaria, at Edificio Arca, Calle Los Martínez de Escobar 3, Oficina 7, tel: 928 27 12 59. It opens 10am–1pm weekdays. For other countries' representations, you may have to call Madrid.

If you lose your passport, or run into trouble with the authorities or the police, contact your consulate for advice. Consulates can issue temporary passports for a fee. You will need a statement of loss or theft from the police, plus two passport-size photographs.

> Where is the American/ British consulate? **¿Dónde está el consulado americano/británico?**

## EMERGENCIES *(urgencia)*

The general emergency number is **112**. For the Civil Guard dial 062, for the local police dial 092, for the national police dial 091 and for an ambulance (Cruz Roja) 902 222 292.

There are the following hospitals in Tenerife:

**Playa de las Americas:** Hospiten Sur (tel: 922 75 00 22).

**Puerto de la Cruz:** Hospiten Bellevue (tel: 922 38 35 51), Hospiten Tamaragua (tel: 922 38 05 12; www.hospiten.es).

**Santa Cruz:** Hospital Universitario de Canarias (tel: 922 67 80

> Police **Policía**
> Fire **Fuego**
> Help! **¡Socorro!**
> Stop! **¡Deténgase!**

00), Hospital Nuestra Señora de la Candelaria (tel: 922 60 20 00; www.hospitaldelacandelaria.com), and Hospiten Rambla (tel: 922 29 16 00).

## G

### GAY AND LESBIAN TRAVELLERS

Major resorts in the Canary Islands have developed facilities for gay and lesbian travellers, including dedicated hotels. Check the websites www.gayiberia.com or www.thegaycanaries.com.

### GETTING TO TENERIFE

**By air:** There are many scheduled and cheap flights from nearly all UK airports to Tenerife. The flight time is 3.5–4.5 hours, and the cost around £100–350. Check the web and the travel sections of weekend newspapers. All-in package holidays can be the least expensive way to go. British Airways (www.britishairways.com, tel:0844 493 0787), and the national carrier Iberia (www.iberia.com, tel: 02 036 843 774) also have promotional deals in the UK.

There are no direct flights to Tenerife from the US. Airlines go via major European airports, with the Spanish state airline Iberia (tel: 1-800 772-4642) going via Madrid, from where internal flights connect to all the Canary Islands. Flights can take 12–13 hours and cost from $1,000.

**By ship:** Trasmediterránea (www.trasmediterranea.es) has a limited number of sailings from Cádiz and ferry connections with other Canary Islands. For further details contact: Southern Ferries, 22 Sussex Street, London, SW1V 4RW, tel: 0844 815 7785, www.southernferries.co.uk.

## H

### HEALTH AND MEDICAL CARE

Tap water is safe to drink but can have a tang to it, so people generally prefer to drink bottled water: *con gas* (sparkling) and *sin gas* (still). Remember that water is scarce, so don't waste it

Non-EU visitors should have private medical insurance, and although there are reciprocal arrangements between EU countries, it is advisable for Britons to take out private insurance, too. The ehic card, which entitles EU citizens to free health care, is available in the UK from post offices or online at www.ehic.org.uk. Before being treated it is advisable to check that the doctor is working within the Spanish Health Service.

**Dental treatment** is not generally available under this system, so private insurance is strongly advised.

**Farmacias** (chemists/drugstores) can deal with a number of health problems. They are usually open during normal shopping hours. After hours, at least one per town remains open all night. Called *farmacia de guardia*, its location is posted in the window of all other *farmacias* nearby and printed in the local newspapers. You can check the address of the nearest farmacia de guardia at the website: http://farmaciatenerife.com.

Where's the nearest (all-night) chemist? **¿Dónde está la farmácia (de guardia) más cercana?**
I need a doctor/dentist. **Necesito un médico/dentista.**
an upset stomach **molestias de estómago**
Is this service public or private? **¿Es este servicio público o privado?**

## HOLIDAYS *(día de fiesta)*

In addition to these Spanish national holidays, many purely local and lesser religious and civic holidays are celebrated in various towns.

**1 January** *Año Nuevo* New Year's Day
**6 January** *Epifanía* Epiphany

**I May** *Día del Trabajo* Labour Day

**25 July** *Santiago Apóstol* St James's Day

**15 August** *Asunción/Nuestra Señora de la Candelaria* Assumption

**12 October** *Día de la Hispanidad* Discovery of America Day (Columbus Day)

**I November** *Todos los Santos* All Saints' Day

**6 December** *Día de la Constitución* Constitution Day

**8 December** *Inmaculada Concepción* Immaculate Conception

**25 December** *Navidad* Christmas Day

Movable dates:

*Carnaval* Week of Shrove Tuesday

*Jueves Santo* Maundy Thursday

*Viernes Santo* Good Friday

*Corpus Christi* Corpus Christi

## L

## LANGUAGE

The Spanish spoken in the Canary Islands is a little different from that of the mainland. For instance, islanders don't lisp when they pronounce the letters c or z. The language of the Canaries is spoken with a slight lilt, reminiscent of the Caribbean, and a number of New World words are used. The most common are *guagua* (pronounced wah-wah), meaning bus, and *papa* (potato). In tourist areas German, English and some French is often spoken, or at least understood.

Do you speak English? **¿Habla usted inglés?**
I don't speak Spanish. **No hablo español.**

## LOST PROPERTY *(Objetos perdidos)*

If you lose an item, report the loss to the Municipal Police or the

Guardia Civil (see Police) and retain a copy of their report for insurance purposes.

> I've lost my wallet/ pocketbook/passport. **He perdido mi cartera/bolso/pasaporte.**

## M

### MAPS

Maps are generally available from hotel receptions and tourist offices, though walking maps are less easy to come by, and should be purchased before going to the area in which you plan to walk.

### MEDIA

**Radio and television** *(radio; televisión)*: Most hotels have international TV channels, including English-language news.

**Newspapers and periodicals**: Many major British and continental papers are on sale on the day of publication. There are a number of unevenly distributed English-language publications with Canarian news and tourist information. These include *Island Connections*, the main English newspaper, *Tenerife News*, a fortnightly paper, also available on the web (www.tenerifenews.com), the online *Tenerife Magazine* (www.tenerifemagazine.com) and the monthly *Revista Living Tenerife* style magazine.

### MONEY MATTERS

**Currency**: The monetary unit in the Canary Islands is the euro (€). Bank notes are available in denominations of 500, 200, 100, 50, 20, 10 and 5. The euro is subdivided into 100 cents and there are coins available for €1 and €2 and for 50, 20, 10, 5, 2 and 1 cent.

**Currency exchange**. Banks are the best place to exchange currency. *Casas de cambio* (exchange offices) stay open outside banking hours.

All larger hotels will also change guests' money, but the rate is less favourable than at the bank. Always take your passport when you go to change money.

**Credit cards**. Major cards are widely recognised on Tenerife, although smaller businesses tend to prefer cash. Visa/Eurocard/MasterCard are the cards that are most generally accepted. Credit and debit cards are also useful for obtaining cash from ATMs, which are to be found in all towns and resorts. They offer the most convenient way of obtaining cash and will usually give you the best exchange rate.

**Travellers' cheques**. Hotels, shops, restaurants and travel agencies all cash travellers' cheques, as do banks, where you are likely to get a better rate (you will need to show your passport).

Where's the nearest bank (currency exchange office)?
**¿Dónde está el banco (la oficina de cambio) más cercana?**
I want to change some dollars/pounds. **Quiero cambiar dólares/libres esterlina.**
Do you accept travellers' cheques? **¿Acepta usted cheques de viajero?**
Can I pay with this credit card? **¿Puedo pagar con esta tarjeta de crédito?**

**O**

## OPENING HOURS

Shops, offices and other businesses generally observe the afternoon siesta, opening from Monday to Saturday 10am–1.30 pm and 5–8.30pm (some on Saturday morning only). In tourist areas many places stay open all day. Post offices are open 8.30–2pm. Banks are open 8.30am–2pm Mon–Fri, with some also open on the occasional afternoon or Saturday morning from Oct–June. Shopping malls are open 9.30am–10pm.

# P

## POLICE (policía)

There are three police forces in Tenerife, as in the rest of Spain. The *Guardia Civil* (Civil Guard) is the main force. Each town also has its own *Policía Municipal* (municipal police), whose uniform varies depending on the town and season but is mostly a combination of blue and grey. The third force, the *Cuerpo Nacional de Policía*, is a national anti-crime unit whose officers wear a light-brown uniform. All police officers are armed.

> Where is the nearest police station? **¿Dónde está la comisaría más cercana?**

## POST OFFICES (correos)

As well as at post offices, stamps *(sellos)* are sold at any tobacconist's *(estancos)* and by most shops selling postcards. Mailboxes are painted yellow. Slots marked *extranjero* are for letters abroad.

> Where is the (nearest) post office? **¿Dónde está la oficina de correos (más cercana)?**
> A stamp for this letter/postcard, please. **Por favor, un sello para esta carta/tarjeta.**

## PUBLIC TRANSPORT

**Airlines:** A number of airlines fly between the islands, and are not much more expensive than ferries. Binter Canarias (www. bintercanarias.com, tel: 902 39 13 92), a subsidiary of Iberia, runs the most flights.

**Bus services:** Buses *(guaguas)* are run by titsa (Transporte Inter-
urbanos de Tenerife SA, www.titsa.com, tel: 922 531 300) and are
frequent, fast and cheap. They cover all major and most minor destinations on the island. Tickets can be bought on board, but if you buy
a BonoVía card from newsagents or some shops beforehand, you get
up to half-price travel on all bus routes. Timetables can be obtained
at bus depots, tourist offices or online.

**Tram services:** The tram service connecting Santa Cruz and La
Laguna is clean, efficient and a good way of avoiding traffic. Ticket
prices start at €1.35 for a single journey. See www.metrotenerife.com
for timetables.

**Ferry services:** Fred Olsen Lines' jetfoil takes 1 hour to Agaete on
Gran Canaria, where there is a free connecting bus to Las Palmas, tak-
ing another hour. Fred Olsen also serves the islands of La Gomera, La
Palma and El Hierro from Los Cristianos. Further information from
Fred Olsen sa (www.fredolsen.es, tel: 902 10 01 07). Note that if you
have bought your ticket in advance, it must be confirmed at the desk
half an hour before departure. Naviera Armas (www.navieraarmas.
com, call centre: 902 45 65 00) runs ferries from Los Cristianos to La
Gomera, La Palma, El Hierro and from Santa Cruz to all the other
Canary Islands. Trasmediterránea (www.trasmediterranea.es, tel: 902
45 46 45) runs ferries to Gran Canaria, taking 2.5 hours for the crossing and other islands.

**T**

## TAXIS

The letters SP *(servicio público)* on the front and rear bumpers of
a car indicate that it is a taxi; it might also have a green light in
the front windscreen or a green sign indicating *'libre'* when it is
free. Fixed prices are displayed on a board at the main taxi rank,
giving the fares to the most popular destinations. In general taxis,
which are easily found in urban areas, provide an inexpensive

method of transport. If in doubt about the fare, ask the driver before setting off.

> **How much is it to Hotel Mencey/the town centre? ¿Cuanto es al Hotel Mencey/al centro?**

## TELEPHONES *(teléfono)*

Most phone booths *(kioskos)* take cards *(tarjetas telefónicas)* available from tobacconists. Instructions in English, along with area codes for different countries, are displayed clearly. For international direct dialling, wait for the dial tone, then dial 00, wait for a second tone and dial the country code, area code (minus the initial zero) and number. In some places there are *cabinas*, phone cabins where you make your call and pay afterwards.

Calling directly from your hotel room is expensive unless you are using a calling card, or a similar system, from a long-distance supplier. Find out from the supplier which free connection number is applicable to Spain (they are different for each country) before you leave, as these numbers are not always easily available once there.

Check with your service provider before leaving home to see if your mobile phone will operate from Tenerife. For more see www. telefonica.es.

**Operator:** The number for the international operator is 025.

**Country codes:** For the US and Canada dial 1, Great Britain 44, Australia 61, New Zealand 64, the Republic of Ireland 353 and South Africa 27.

**Local codes:** The code for Spain is +34. For the Canary Islands a prefix must always be dialled, even for local calls: Province of Santa Cruz de Tenerife (Tenerife, El Hierro, La Gomera and La Palma) 922; Province of Las Palmas de Gran Canaria (Gran Canaria, Lanzarote and Fuerteventura) 928.

## TIME DIFFERENCES

In winter the Canary Islands maintain Greenwich Mean Time, which is one hour behind most European countries, including Spain, but the same as the UK. For the rest of the year the islands go on summer time, as does Spain – keeping the one-hour difference.

Winter time chart:

| Los Angeles | New York | London | **Canaries** | Madrid |
|---|---|---|---|---|
| 4am | 7am | noon | **noon** | 1pm |

## TIPPING (*propinas*)

Since a service charge is often included in restaurant bills, tipping is not obligatory. Ten percent of the bill is usual for taxi drivers, bar staff, waiters and hairdressers. Also tip porters and maids a few euros, depending on your length of stay.

## TOILETS

The most commonly used expressions for toilets in the Canaries are *servicios* or *aseos*, though you may also hear or see WC ('doobla-vay say') and *retretes*. Public conveniences are located by most beaches. Hotels, bars and restaurants usually have lavatories and it is considered polite to buy a coffee if you do drop in to use their facilities.

Where are the lavatories? **¿Dónde están los servicios?**

## TOURIST INFORMATION

Obtain information on the Canary Islands from www.spain.info or from **Spanish National Tourist Offices,** which include the following:

**Canada:** 2 Bloor Street West, 34th Floor, Toronto, Ontario M4W 3E2, tel: (416) 961-3131, email: toronto@tourspain.es.

**UK:** 6th floor, 64 North Row, London W1K 7DE, tel: 020 7317 2010 (visits by appointment), email: londres@tourspain.es.

**Ireland:** 1, Westmoreland Street, Dublin 2, tel: 0818 462960 for information and brochure requests, email: dublin@tourspain.es.

**US:** Chicago: Water Tower Place, Suite 915 East 845, North Michigan Avenue, Chicago, il 60611, tel: (312) 642-1992, email: chicago@tourspain.es.

Los Angeles: 8383 Wilshire Boulevard, Suite 960, Beverly Hills, Los Angeles, ca 90211, tel: (323) 658 7188, email: losangeles@tourspain.es.

New York: 60 East 42nd Street, Suite 5300 (53rd Floor),, New York, ny 10103, email: nuevayork@tourspain.es.

For questions on Tenerife you can call the official tourist helpline 00-800-100-101-00 free of charge. Information is available in English, German and French (9am–5pm Mon–Fri).

The main office for the whole island is the Cabildo Insular in Plaza de España, Santa Cruz de Tenerife, tel: 922 28 93 94, Mon–Fri 9am–6pm (5pm July–Sept), Sat 9am–1pm (noon July–Sep). The Tenerife tourist board has three websites: www.webtenerife.com, www.tenerife.es and www.todotenerife.es.

Information may also be obtained from the following **local tourist information offices:**

**Aeropuerto Tenerife-Norte** (Arrivals Terminal): tel: 922 82 50 46; Mon–Fri 9am–5pm.

**Aeropuerto Tenerife-Sur Reina Sofia** (Arrivals Terminal): tel: 922 39 20 37; Mon–Fri 9am–9pm, till 5pm on Sat–Sun, July–Sept Mon–Fri 9am–7pm, till 5pm on Sat–Sun.

**Costa Adeje:** Avenida Rafael Puig 17, tel: 922 75 06 33; Mon–Fri 10am–5pm, till 4pm July–Sept.

**La Laguna:** Calle La Carrera 7, Bajo, Casa de Alvaredo Bracamonte, tel: 922 63 11 94; daily 9am–5pm.

**La Orotava:** Calle Calvario 4, tel: 922 32 30 41; Mon–Fri 8.30am–6pm.

**Los Cristianos:** Centro Cultural (Casa de La Cultura), Plaza de Pescador, tel: 922 75 71 37; Mon–Fri 9am–3.30pm, Sat 9am–1pm.

**Playa de las Américas, Arona:** Avenida Rafael Puig 1, tel: 922 79 76 68; Mon–Fri 9am–9pm, Sat–Sun 9am–3.30pm.

**Puerto de la Cruz:** Casa de la Aduana, Calle Las Lonjas, tel: 922 38 60 00; Oct–Jun Mon–Fri 9am–8pm, Sat–Sun 9am–5pm, July–Sept Mon–Fri 9am–7pm, Sat–Sun 9am–5pm.

## TRAVELLERS WITH DISABILITIES

Tenerife is well adapted to the needs of travellers with disabilities. There are wheelchair ramps at the major airports and many larger apartments and hotels make provision for disabled guests. Some of the more modern resorts also provide ramps to cross pavements. The facilities at Los Cristianos are renowned among disabled travellers. Access Travel (www.access-travel.co.uk) in the UK (tel: 01942 888 844) offers holidays for the disabled.

Wheelchairs can be hired from Ortopedia Hospitalaria Lero, Puerto De La Cruz (tel: 922 75 02 89) or Orange Badge (www.orangebadge.eu, tel: 922 79 73 55).

## W

## WEBSITES

There are Internet cafés in the main towns and resorts. The following websites have useful, up-to-date information about Tenerife:
www.spain.info Spanish tourist office website
www.turismodecanarias.com Canary Islands tourism website
www.webtenerife.com Tourist office site in several languages
www.ecoturismocanarias.com Rural tourism accommodation
www.tenerifetimes.com Blog and information site
www.tenerifemagazine.com Lively, informative online magazine

## Recommended Hotels

This selection of hotels is designed to give a cross section of accommodation available in the main towns (for details of accommodation in general, see page 116). It's best to book in advance, particularly in high season or at carnival time, when prices go up. High season is November to February, July and August. Don't expect to find accommodation everywhere – it is mainly concentrated in the larger towns and resorts. As a basic guide to room prices we have used the following symbols for a double room with bath/shower in high season:

€€€€ over 160 euros
€€€ 90–160 euros
€€ 65–90 euros
€ under 65 euros

## THE NORTHEAST

## ANAGA

**Albergue Montes de Anaga €** *tel: 922 82 20 56*, www.albergues tenerife.com. This modern, three-storey block with 8 bedrooms (sleeping between 2 and 6 people) is just about the only place to stay in the middle of the Parque Rural de Anaga. Fabulously set in a remote location, with impressive views, it is walker-friendly, and you can also hire bikes here and get information about the park. Meals and picnics are available.

## LA LAGUNA

**Aguere €€** *Calle Obispo Rey Redondo 55, tel: 922 31 40 36*, www. hotelaguere.es. This mansion, situated in the middle of the unesco World Heritage quarter of town, was at one time the home of the bishop of Tenerife. It became a hotel in 1885 and passed into the present family's hands in 1920. There are 23 en-suite bedrooms and free WiFi, but its facilities only merit one star, hence its wonderful value.

**Casa Rural La Asomada del Gato** € *Calle Anchieta 45, tel: 922 26 39 37*, www.laasomadadelgato.es. A rustic house in the historic centre of town. Book well in advance for there are only four rooms and they are excellent value. Each has its own bathroom and faces on to the central courtyard, and there's a dining room for hotel guests.

**Nivaria** €€€ *Plaza del Adelantado 11, tel: 922 26 42 98*, www.hotel nivaria.com. Situated in the main square of the old town, this hotel is based on an 18th-century mansion, with a new block behind. The former apartments have all been fully refurbished and converted to guest rooms and suites. Some parking is available.

## SANTA CRUZ

**Iberostar Mencey** €€€€ *Doctor José Navéiras 38, tel: 922 60 99 00*, www.iberostar.com. Old-fashioned luxury in the heart of town, close to the parliament, and frequented by government officials and visiting dignitaries. There is a tennis court, casino, swimming pool and a top-notch restaurant.

**Pension Cejas** €€ *Calle de San Francisco 47, tel: 922 281 872;* www. pensioncejas.com. Conveniently located in the heart of the old quarter, just a short walk from Plaza de España and the harbour, this family-run colonial guest house offers single, double and triple rooms and two beautiful indoor gardens. Free WiFi.

**Adonis Hotel Plaza** €€ *Plaza de la Candelaria 10, tel: 922 27 24 53*, www.adonisresorts.com. Efficiently run and situated right in the heart of the pedestrian shopping streets by the port, this 3-star hotel is suited for business as well as leisure. Free WiFi area.

## THE NORTH

## EL TEIDE

**Parador de Cañadas del Teide** €€€ *38300 La Orotava, tel: 922 38 64 15*, www.paradores.es. This parador has a stunning setting directly under El Teide and close to the cable car, and is decorated in Canary Islands style. It's worth dropping in for a coffee or meal if you are not staying. Guests can watch the sun rise over the volcano and beat the cable-car crowds. Has 37 rooms and a pool, sauna and gym. Best to opt for half board.

## LA OROTAVA

**Hotel Rural Orotava €€** *Calle Carrera Escultor Estevez 17, tel: 922 32 27 93*, http://hotelruralorotava.es. An attractive converted mansion in the centre of the old town, with comfortable rooms. Attached is Sabor Canario, a restaurant serving traditional food in a leafy courtyard setting.

**Pensión Silene €** *Calle Tomás Zerolo 9, tel: 922 33 01 99*; www.silene orotava.es. Feel at home in this elegant *pensión* in a 19th-century town house.

**Victoria €€€** *Hermano Apolinar 8, tel: 922 33 16 83*, www.hotelrural victoria.com. A gorgeously restored 16th-century mansion in the old quarter, with a fine view from the roof terrace. The restaurant has good local dishes and wines. 14 rooms.

## LOS REALEJOS

**Maritim HotelTenerife €€€** *El Burgado, tel: 922 37 90 00*, www. maritim.es. This four-star, high-rise hotel is set in a tropical garden, just outside Puerto de la Cruz, and has a pool and terrace overlooking the sea. Rooms are functional, with good views. Entertainment is laid on and there is a free bus into town 15 minutes' ride away.

## PUERTO DE LA CRUZ

**4Dreams Hotel €** *Agustín Bethencourth 14, tel: 922 38 35 52*, www.4 dreamshotel.com. A modern, small, competitvely-priced hotel in a pedestrianised street a few minutes from Plaza del Charco. Pool and solarium boast magnificent sea views. 62 rooms.

**Beatriz Atlantis & Spa €€€** *Avenida Venezuela 15, tel: 922 37 45 45,* www.beatrizhoteles.com. Completely refurbished and close to the beach, this large block has 320 rooms, a good-sized swimming pool and a new state-of-the-art spa with fine views of the sea and Mount Teide.

**Hotel Botánico and Oriental Spa Garden €€€€** *Avenida Richard J. Yeoward 1, tel: 922 38 14 00,* www.hotelbotanico.com. Set in tropical gardens and parklands, this five-star luxury hotel has an elegant and peaceful atmosphere with views over the ocean and Mount Teide. Four restaurants, bars, boutiques, luxury spa and fitness centre. 252 rooms.

**Los Geranios €** *Calle El Lomo 14, tel: 922 38 28 10,* www.pensionlos geranios.com. A clean and pleasant pensión in a quiet street in the old part of town.

**Marquesa €€** *Calle Quintana 11, tel: 922 38 31 51,* www.hotel marquesa.com. This beautiful 1712 mansion has been extended to provide 150 rooms, most with balconies. The terrace at the front of the hotel overlooks the pedestrianised street and is ideal for people-watching. There is a swimming pool and sauna.

**Monopol €€** *Quintana 15, tel: 922 38 46 11,* www.monopoltf.com. Next door but one to the Marquesa (see above), this is an equally handsome mansion and its lovely balconied courtyard makes an elegant lobby. There are 92 rooms with all amenities, as well as a swimming pool and sauna.

**Hotel Rural Bentor €€** *Calle del Cantillo de Abajo 6, Los Realejos, tel: 922 35 34 58,* www.hotelruralbentor.com. In Los Realejos, behind Puerto de la Cruz, this is a blend of the old and the new, the 19 rooms split between a finely renovated 17th-century mansion and a new building beyond the courtyard. Has a pool, solarium, popular bar and restaurant.

**San Telmo €€** *Paseo San Telmo 18, tel: 922 38 58 53.* Right on the seafront, with balconied rooms overlooking the sea, which splashes against the rocks all night long. Not posh, this is a delightful, old-fashioned hotel. A buffet breakfast is included in the price and there's a small rooftop pool.

**Hotel Tigaiga €€€** *Parque Taoro 28, tel: 922 38 35 00,* www.tigaiga. com. Stylish hotel set in tropical garden with amazing views over the town and Teide. 76 spacious and comfortable rooms have full length windows and balconies as well as free WLAN access. There is also a heated outdoor pool and two restaurants.

## THE NORTHWEST

## GARACHICO

**Hotel Gara €€€** *Calle Esteban de Ponte 7, tel: 922 83 11 68,* www. garahotel.com. The 16-room Gara is a restored 18th-century rustic-style house, with fine views of the north coast. Has spa facilities and a spacious terrace.

**Pensión El Jardín €** *Esteban de Ponte 8, tel: 922 83 02 45.* This family-run *pensión* is in an old townhouse with a patio. The bedrooms leading off the first-floor landing have no windows, but are spacious and comfortable with original furniture. The large family attic room has rooftop views. The hotel can also organise diving trips.

**La Quinta Roja €€€** *Glorieta de San Francisco s/n, tel: 922 13 33 77,* www.quintaroja.com. This lovely mansion in the quiet central square is a survivor of the 18th-century earthquake. It was home of the Marqués of Quinta Roja and is typical of island baroque style. It is very well connected to local activities, organising excursions into the countryside.

**Hotel Rural El Patio €€€** *Finaca Malpaís El Guincho, tel: 922 13 32 80,* www.hotelpatio.com. Inland and just east of Garachico, this inviting hotel is on a banana plantation in a house that is said to date from the 16th century. There are 26 bedrooms decorated in rural style. Walks head off through the gardens and plantations and there is a heated pool and restaurant.

**Hotel San Roque €€€€** *Calle Esteban de Ponte 32, tel: 922 13 34 35,* www.hotelsanroque.com. This 18th-century mansion in the centre of town has a warm, stylish interior and wonderful views of Teide.

Rooms come with designer furniture and contemporary local art. There is a swimming pool, sauna and rooftop solarium.

## THE SOUTH

## EL MÉDANO

**Hotel Médano €€–€€€** *Paseo Picacho 2, tel: 922 17 70 00, www. medano.es.* On the beach with four sun terraces, overlooking the sea and the Montaña Roja. Offers windsurfing, kitesurfing, scuba diving, trekking, cycling and golf.

**Playa Sur Tenerife €€€** *E-38612 El Medano, tel: 922 17 61 20, www. hotelplayasurtenerife.com.* Isolated in the middle of a long stretch of beach, this has long been a windsurfers' choice, with boards for hire. All rooms have balconies with views. There is a pool, sauna, restaurant and bar.

## GRANADILLA DE ABONA

**Hotel Rural Senderos de Abona €€€** *Calle de la Iglesia 5, tel: 922 77 02 00, www.senderosdeabona.es.* An enclosed hotel that was once the post office, in the quiet streets of Granadilla. The rooms are individually furnished and there is a good restaurant, as well as a collection of tools and implements in a 'museum'. Only the clock on the church opposite disturbs the peace, every quarter of an hour.

## GÜÍMAR

**Casona Santo Domingo €€** *Calle Santo Domingo 32, tel: 922 51 02 29, www.casonasantodomingo.com.* An elegant, central hotel rural dating from the 16th century, with pitch pine balconies, period furniture and a common sitting room containing coffee-table books about the area. The restaurant serves a menu of local dishes.

**Hotel Rural Finca Salamanca €€€** *Carretera Güimar–El Puertito, Km1.5, tel: 922 51 45 30, www.hotel-fincasalamanca.com.* A manor house, in a country estate, that has been converted into a charming small hotel for those who want peace and quiet as well as top-class facilities. There are 20 rooms, including bungalows, a restaurant, heated pool and botanic gardens.

## THE SOUTHWEST

## ADEJE

**Dream Gran Tacande €€€** *Calle Alcalde Walter Paetzmann s/n*, tel: 922 74 64 00, www.dreamplacehotels.com. One of the Dreamplace resorts that tries to look like a swanky village, built in various Canarian architectural styles. There's a heated salt-water pool and 207 rooms, plus the Royal or Imperial suites with their own Jacuzzis.

**La Fonda Central €€** *Calle Grande 26, tel: 922 781 550;* www.fondacentral.es. An attractive noble house, with courtyard, dating from the 18th century, situated in the old part of town. The hotel has 11 en-suite rooms, a solarium, bar and restaurant.

**Gran Hotel Bahía del Duque Resort €€€€** *Avenida Bruselas tel: 922 74 69 00,* www.bahia-duque.com. A vast luxury complex reminiscent of Disneyland with its multicoloured mini-chateaux set among 63,000 square metres of exotic gardens leading to the beach. Forty new villas opened in 2008, each with its own infinity-style pool. The extensive facilities include a spa and nine themed restaurants.

## LOS CRISTIANOS

**Hotel Andrea's €€** *Avenida Valle Menéndez 6, tel: 922 79 00 12,* www.hotelesreveron.com. One of the few non four-star hotels in Los Cristianos, this modern hotel is clean, friendly and good value. Try to get a room overlooking the street as inner rooms are a bit gloomy. No breakfast, but connected to a downstairs pizza restaurant.

**Spring Arona Gran Hotel €€€€** *Avenida Juan Carlos I 38, tel: 922 75 06 78,* www.springhoteles.com. On a slightly scrubby stretch of beach at the end of Los Cristianos harbour, this hotel has 400 modern rooms and a terrace overlooking the water. Features sports facilities, restaurants and bars, and a wonderful atrium lobby bedecked with green plants hanging from each floor.

## PLAYA DE LAS AMÉRICAS

**Flamingo Suites €€€€** *Avenida España 6, tel: 922 71 84 00*, www. flamingosuites.co.uk. These luxury apartments in the heart of Playa de las Américas are considered Tenerife's most exclusive private club. They have every modern facility, including Jacuzzi tubs, plunge pools and daily maid service. Sixteen villas and two suites.

**Mare Nostrum Resort €€€** *Avenida de las Américas s/n, tel: 922 75 75 45*, http://marenostrumresort.expohotels.com. Choose from one of five 5-star hotels in this classical fantasy land – Sir Anthony, Cleopatra Palaceand Mediterranean Palace (with rooftop nudist zone and pool). Together they provide hundreds of rooms, some with their own private pools, with thalassotherapy a speciality, and numerous restaurants.

## VILAFLOR

**Hotel El Nogal €€€** *Camino Real s/n La Escalona, tel: 922 72 60 50*, www.hotelnogal.com. This secluded 19th-century estate between Arona and Vilaflor has been converted into a hotel by its owners, descendants of the orginal Linares family. There are 42 rooms tastefully furnished.

**Hotel El Sombrerito €–€€** *Calle Santa Catalina 15, tel: 922 70 90 52*,. Enjoy traditional Canarian hospitality at this 210-room, family-run *pensión*. The restored inn is decorated with rural artefacts and the hotel's restaurant serves local cuisine. You can even feed their goats.

**VillAlba Spa Hotel €€** *Camino San Roque s/n, tel: 922 70 99 30*, www.hotelvillalba.com. 'The highest hotel in Spain' is the boast of this modern hotel 1,660m (5,450ft) above sea level. There are 27 rooms with stunning views, a spa pool and gym. Many activities are available through the hotel, including hang-gliding, mountain biking and climbing.

# INDEX

**A**deje 75
Aguamansa 58
Anaga Hills 39
Arguayo 69

**B**ajamar 39
Boca de Tauce 62
Bosque de Esperanza 58

**C**amello Center 68
Candelaria 80
Casa de la Miel 51
Casa del Vino La Baranda 50
Chinamada 41
Costa del Silencio 76
Cueva del Hermano Pedro 77

**E**l Médano 76
El Tanque 68
El Teide 54
El Teno Rural Park 62
Erjos 69

**F**aro del Teno 66

**G**arachico
    Mirador de Garachico 64
    Plaza de Juan Gonzales de la Torre 64
    Santa Ana church 65
Granadilla de Abona 78
    Museo de la Historia de Granadilla de Abona 78
Guía de Isora 70
Güímar 79

**I**cod de los Vinos 52

El Drago Milenario 52
    Mariposario del Drago 53
Isla Baja 63

**L**a Caleta 73
La Esperanza 58
La Gomera 74
La Laguna 36
    Ayuntamiento 36, 48
    Convento de Santa Clara de Asis 38
    Iglesia de la Concepción 37
    Museo Antropología de Tenerife 38
    Palacio de Nava 36
    Plaza del Adelantado 36
La Orotava 47
    Casa de los Balcones 48
    Iglesia de Nuestra Señora de la Concepción 49
    Jardínes Marquesado de la Quinta Roja 47
    Museo de Cerámica 48
    San Agustín church 47
Las Galletas 76
La Tejita 76
Los Cristianos 73
Los Gigantes 69
Los Organos 58
Los Realejos 52
Los Roques de García 60

**M**arguerita de Piedra 58
Masca 67

Mirador de Don Martín 78
Mirador de El Boquerón 39
Mirador del Pico del Inglés 40
Montaña del Chinyero 69
Montaña Roja 76
Montañas de Anaga 40
Montañeta del Palmer 67

**O**bservatorio Astronómico del Teide 59
Observatorio Meteorológico de Izaña 59
Orotava Valley 41

**P**arque Etnográfico Pirámides de Güímar 78
Parque Nacional de las Cañadas del Teide 54
Parque Rural Anaga 40
Playa de las Américas 73
    Baranco del Rey 72
Playa La Caleta de Interián 66
Playa San Marcos 54
Playa San Roque 40
Puertito de Güímar 80
Puerto de la Cruz 42
    Ábaco Casa Museo 46
    Ermita de San Juan Batista 43
    Iglesia de Nuestra Señora de la Peña de Francia 43
    Iglesia de San Francisco 43
    Jardín Botánico 46

Loro Parque 44
promenade 45
Puerto Santiago 70
Punto Hidalgo 39

**S**an Cristóbal de la. *See* La
Laguna
San Juan 70
San Juan de la Rambla 52
Santa Catalina church 52
Santa Cruz 27
Cabildo Insular 29
Calle del Castillo 29

Iglesia de San
Francisco 30
Monumento a los
Caídos 28
Museo de la
Naturaleza y el
Hombre 31
Museo Militar
Regional de
Canarias 34
Museo Municipal de
Bellas Artes 29
Nuestra Señora de la

Concepción 30
Parque Marítimo
César Manrique 33
Plaza Candelaria 29
Plaza de España 28
Rambla 33

**T**acoronte 51
Tacoronte-Acentejo wine
area 50
Teleférico 59

**V**ilaflor 61

**Berlitz** pocket guide

# Tenerife

**Fourth Edition 2015**

**Editor:** Sarah Clark
**Author:** Maciej Zglinicki, Roger Williams
**Head of Production:** Rebeka Davies
**Update Production:** AM Services
**Pictures:** Richard Cooke
**Cartography Update:** Carte
**Photography Credits:** Getty Images 18, 22;
iStock 66; Public domain 21; Shutterstock 1,
2TC, 2TL, 2MC, 2ML, 3T, 3TC, 3M, 3M, 3M, 3M,
4ML, 4ML, 4MR, 4TL, 4TL, 4/5B, 5MC, 5T, 5TC,
6TL, 6ML, 6ML, 7MC, 7MC, 7TC, 8, 10, 11, 13,
14, 17, 19, 24, 26, 28, 30, 31, 33, 34, 35, 37, 38,
39, 41, 42, 44, 45, 46, 47, 48, 50, 51, 53, 55, 56,
58, 60, 61, 62, 63, 64, 65, 67, 68, 69, 71, 72, 75,
76, 77, 78, 79, 80, 81, 82, 84, 85, 87, 89, 90, 91,
93, 94, 96, 98, 99, 100, 102, 103, 105
**Cover Picture:** AWL Images

**Distribution**

**UK:** Dorling Kindersley Ltd,
A Penguin Group company, 80 Strand, London,
WC2R 0RL; sales@uk.dk.com
**United States:** Ingram Publisher Services,
1 Ingram Boulevard, PO Box 3006, La Vergne,
TN 37086-1986; ips@ingramcontent.com
**Australia and New Zealand:** Woodslane,
10 Apollo St, Warriewood, NSW 2102,
Australia; info@woodslane.com.au

**Worldwide:** Apa Publications (Singapore) Pte,
7030 Ang Mo Kio Avenue 5,
08-65 Northstar @ AMK, Singapore 569880
apasin@singnet.com.sg

All Rights Reserved
© 2015 Apa Digital (CH) AG and
Apa Publications (UK) Ltd

Berlitz Trademark Reg. U.S. Patent Office and
other countries. Marca Registrada. Used under
licence from the Berlitz Investment Corporation

Printed in China by CTPS

No part of this book may be reproduced,
stored in a retrieval system or transmitted
in any form or means electronic, mechanical,
photocopying, recording or otherwise, without
prior written permission from Apa Publications.

**Contact us**

Every effort has been made to provide accurate
information in this publication, but changes are
inevitable. The publisher cannot be responsible
for any resulting loss, inconvenience or injury.
We would appreciate it if readers would
call our attention to any errors or outdated
information. We also welcome your suggestions;
please contact us at: berlitz@apaguide.co.uk
www.insightguides.com/berlitz

# Berlitz®

speaking your language

**phrase book & dictionary**
**phrase book & CD**

**Available in**: Arabic, Brazilian Portuguese*, Burmese*, Cantonese
Chinese, Croatian, Czech*, Danish*, Dutch, English, Filipino, Finnish*, French,
German, Greek, Hebrew*, Hindi*, Hungarian*, Indonesian, Italian, Japanese,
Korean, Latin American Spanish, Malay, Mandarin Chinese, Mexican Spanish,
Norwegian, Polish, Portuguese, Romanian*, Russian, Spanish, Swedish, Thai,
Turkish, Vietnamese
*Book only